Reel Vision

Unlocking Metaphysical Meaning in Movies

Volume 1

By Robert Capozzi

With Cynthia Bové

Reel Vision

ISBN: 978-0692310182

For additional information, please visit www.reel-vision.webs.com

GNOSIS
PRESS

Bellport, NY

Contents

Reel Vision

Foreword/Acknowledgements

It is an audacious act to write a book. One might think one has something more to offer, some angle, some insight, something that will sell, even if it's only a fleeting, semi-formed idea.

Especially in the non-fiction category, books sometimes can be an extension of a career. For example, a clinical psychologist might write a self-help-type book as an outgrowth of his or her practice. Chefs might write cookbooks. That sort of thing.

Not the case here. My life story is probably not all that interesting to most, not even my closest friends and family! Still, the way I figure it, were I going to spend a few hours with this book, I'd want to know – in summary – where the author is coming from. I'd like to have a sense of whether he's got the credentials and the chops to spend time reading his words.

The subtitle tells you this is a work about "movies," and it also tells you it is about "metaphysics." I'm guessing that you wouldn't be reading this if you didn't have at least some interest in both subjects.

The movies deconstructed in this first volume – *The Matrix, Dark City, Inception, Revolver,* and *Vanilla Sky* – are also listed on the cover, so one or more of those may have caught your eye.

Now, a brief history of how this book project came about. I'm a middle-aged dude from the greater New York area. College educated, pre-law with a minor in journalism. Editor of the campus weekly news magazine. Accepted to law school, but opted to go for a Master's in economics, which I didn't quite finish.

After undergrad, moved to the Washington, D.C., area to work in politics. Later, I transitioned to the corporate world, where I was an executive in the wild world of Wall Street and investor relations during the booming times of the burgeoning tech, telecom, and Internet fields during the 1990s.

The upshot of all this is I made just enough money to semi-retire in my early 40s.

On a separate track, one of my best friends back in college was a brilliant guy named Peter who, after undergrad, went to graduate school for screenwriting. That was cool enough, but Peter went to UCLA, one of the – if not *the* – best film schools in the nation.

I got the idea that I could write screenplays, too, although I viewed it as a hobby that maybe one day could turn into something more. Peter recommended books on the subject. I wrote a few screen- and teleplays in my spare time. After a few attempts, Peter said, "Robert, you are an excellent writer, but you don't know how to write a screenplay."

You might think screenwriting is not that hard, but, take my word for it, it's tough, tough work. It's definitely *not* a hobby.

1

Just prior to my decision to semi-retire, I had – for lack of a better term – a profound spiritual experience. I won't go into the details, but suffice it to say that my life went on a markedly different trajectory. Since I was semi-retired, I had plenty of time to read. I immersed myself in spiritual works, from *A Course in Miracles* (ACIM), to Indian sages like Ramana Maharshi and Nisargadatta Maharaj, to the *Tao Te Ching,* to more pop offerings like Eckhart Tolle and Deepak Chopra, or more obscure truth-tellers like Jed McKenna.

Since I'd given up trying to *write* movies, I did the next best thing: I watched them. I probably watched at least four films a week. For six years, I was a full-time student of metaphysical spirituality and movies. An informal student, to be sure, but I certainly feel I learned a lot in those years.

A former live-in girlfriend, Lesley Kelly, kept in touch with me after the relationship fizzled. She had similar interests in spirituality and film, and much of our relationship revolved around discussions of both subjects. About a year after she left me for greener pastures, she went on a spiritual retreat with a teacher named David Hoffmeister. I knew of Hoffmeister a bit, and I was impressed by his use of film to help illustrate metaphysical and spiritual insights.

After the retreat, Lesley called me excitedly, saying she'd seen the film *Revolver* at Hoffmeister's recommendation. It's the bomb, she said.

While I'd seen other Guy Ritchie films, I had not heard of this movie by him, *Revolver*. I got a DVD copy, and was almost instantly mesmerized by the flick. But it all went by so fast, I wasn't really sure what the movie was all about.

So, I watched it again, sometimes pausing it to take notes. Still not totally getting it, I watched it yet again. I started sharing emails with Lesley on the film's deeper meanings. After this informal dialog, I decided that this *Revolver* needed to be completely deconstructed. I did so, creating a website for anyone to stumble upon.

My screenwriter friend Peter read my *Revolver* deconstruction. After some discussion, he suggested that the caliber of my piece was so good that I should do more of these and to package them as a book. And that was the beginning of this project.

I'd since moved back to the New York area. There I met my good friend Cynthia Bové. Not only is she the author of a spiritual book, *The Fifth Disciple*, but she is a certifiable film buff. We kicked around ideas about how the book should be structured, which films should be included, and so forth. During the writing of this book, Cynthia was kind enough to provide feedback and editing suggestions, pretty much from start to finish. Her contributions were so significant that she earned a "with" byline.

Lesley and Peter also provided extensive, insightful feedback on the project. Thank you all!

Obviously, taste in film is highly subjective. I feel good about the choices I made picking these as the first five films. My intention is to continue to write these long-form deconstructions in future volumes in this series, films like *What Dreams May Come, Groundhog Day, The Wizard of Oz,* and so many more. I'd appreciate it greatly if you as the reader would provide feedback on my website not only on the films that I have deconstructed here but films that you would like to see in future volumes. Go to: www.reel-vision.webs.com.

Similarly, you may not agree with some of my interpretations of these films, but hopefully you will find some nugget of insight that will inspire you on the journey. Frankly, in a year, I might either find obvious understandings that I missed or even disagree with my own interpretations of these flicks, so, no worries, mate! *Reel Vision*, is *a way,* not *the way,* to look at metaphysical spirituality in film.

I do hope you enjoy reading this book as much as I did writing it.

Robert Capozzi
Bellport, NY

Introduction

NOTE: Readers may choose to read this Introduction first, which sets the stage for the book by offering a theory of the "metaphysical movie"; why such films are so rich and satisfying; and some other insights that you might find helpful. Others may prefer to dive into the deconstructions of these first five flicks, then circle back to this Introduction to pull the whole book together.

It's your choice. It always is.

Then the question becomes: Should one have viewed all five of these films *prior to* or *after* reading *Reel Vision*. Once again, it depends. Either can work. Some may have seen *The Matrix*, *Inception*, and *Vanilla Sky*, but not *Dark City* or *Revolver*, for example. View the ones you've not seen before or after reading this book. It's all good.

It *is* recommended to see all five films, to be sure. Unlike me, you may not need to watch these films multiple times to "get" them, hopefully at least with the help of this book you may not need to!

Perhaps the reader has seen one or more of these films, and not enjoyed the experience. That's OK. I liked *The Matrix* the first time, but I didn't recognize it for the work of genius that I do now. I found *Vanilla Sky* confusing and not all that appealing. And *Inception* I liked initially but also found it confusing as well.

The more obscure films – *Dark City* and *Revolver* – I did like on first viewing, although it was no surprise to me that they were not big box-office winners. And I certainly didn't really see them as brilliant artworks that I do now.

In writing this book, I've probably watched all five of these movies five times or more. Candidly, I didn't really understand these films until the second or third viewings, with the possible exception of *The Matrix*.

In some ways – again except for *The Matrix* – these are not so much "films" but "filmic experiences." That is, these films tend to not be linear. Sometimes, viewers may struggle with following the storylines of these flicks. Including *The Matrix*, there is a lot of encoded symbolism and nuanced storytelling in all five of these movies.

Proceed with ~~caution~~ reckless abandon!

Toward a Theory of the Metaphysical Movie

Film is not philosophy, metaphysics, or spirituality. And yet, in a different sense, film *reflects* a philosophical perspective, but only because *everything* is philosophy. Our beliefs, emotions, assumptions, and perceptions give meaning to all that we behold. The physical universe is neutral unto itself; it has no inherent meaning.

There's no getting around it. From the moment we wake, one's conscious mind is making thousands of judgments and assessments. We open our eyes while stretching an arm to choose whether to turn off the alarm or press the snooze button. Even in the fog of the first few minutes after rising, we already are aware of what mood we are in, whether we are charged up and ready for the day, or whether we had a bad dream, didn't sleep well, or whatever other cross we may bear.

Behind all these judgments, we have a thought system, a philosophical perspective. We carry this perspective around with us all the day long. We apply our perspectives to everything, from important life decisions to the most mundane aspects of existence.

Consider: "I feel tired" is an assessment based on a perspective, a learned one. The word "tired" is a word we use to describe a feeling of tiredness. The word itself is not the *feeling* of being tired; they are different things. If I feel tired when I first rise in the morning, I may make an assessment: Get out of bed because I have important things to do, or, stay in bed for 15 more minutes to more gently ease into the day, there's time for it, anyway, etc., etc., etc.

You might be asking, "What does this have to do with film?" The point is that filmmakers, as human beings, unavoidably have philosophical perspectives, too, because we all do. Filmmakers make millions of decisions about the storyline, casting, the sets, and the music that go into the plus-or-minus-two-hours of sounds and images that we call a "movie." It seems almost absurd, but these movies can sometimes exceed $100 million to produce this stream of sounds and images. On balance, the market for film continues to grow dramatically, despite tremendous technological changes like video streaming that have dropped the average inflation-adjusted price of watching a film.

More than Just Bread & Circuses

In 1947, attendance to the movies in the U.S. was 4.7 billion. The advent of television knocked that down to about 1 billion per year in the 1950s, but still today some Americans will spend $10+ (plus popcorn and a soda) to sit in a darkened theater with strangers at the rate of about 1.5 billion a year. With a population of over 300 million, that means Americans still troop to the movies around five times a year on average.[1]

The global entertainment and media market is expected to top $2 trillion by 2016.[2] Global box-office revenues alone were about $36 billion in 2013.[3] To put that in perspective, the ninth-largest economy (Italy) had a roughly $2 trillion gross domestic product in 2013. And Jordan – the 90th largest economy – had a roughly $34 billion economy in 2013.[4]

As a people, we love entertainment, and can't seem to get enough of movies, television, sports, and video games. We now can see movies in so many venues – in the theater, on television, and even streaming on the Internet. I've been known to watch Netflix on my phone while on the treadmill at the gym, for example.

The question is, why are we so seemingly obsessed with these moving pictures and sounds?

Is it merely "entertainment," a way for us to suspend our belief in our own lives, to go to another place in our mind, where we identify with the characters who are beautiful, rich, strong, vigorous, or funny? Do we wish to be inspired by the valor or romance being played out on the screen? Do we use it to quietly vent our contempt for those who have what we don't, or to feel superior to those whose behavior we don't approve of? Can we relate in some way to the foibles of others, in a kind of misery-loves-company sort of way?

These are all likely scenarios, but this book suggests that we have a deeper motive. On some level, we subconsciously seek validation of our philosophical thought system. More rarely, we recognize that our philosophy-of-life is not really working for us, and we seek inspiration for another way of being.

The film industry is very effective in putting together stories and moods that allow us to suspend our judgment and buy-into the film as something approximating life. Since we have a shared culture, filmmakers exploit our broadly shared philosophical perspectives. We have all learned what "right and wrong" is, so virtually all films have a *protagonist* and an *antagonist*. Unless we are in a sadistic mood, we relate to and pull for the protagonist, and we condemn the antagonist. For films we don't like, we often don't buy-into the protagonist's dilemma and/or character.

Of course, sometimes we also (sometimes secretly) like the villain, too. Perhaps we admire the bad boy's aggressive audacity or derisive wit. Here again, these may be qualities we wish we had in our own arsenal of personality traits.

Film as Soul Food

Many times films inspire us, lifting our spirits. Watching acts of bravery, heroism, and overcoming the odds in films teach us that we can face our fears and can inspire us to be better people for it. In spiritual circles, it's been said in differing ways that there are only two core emotions: love or fear. If so, then prevailing over fear necessarily leads to the emotion of love, which is helpful indeed. If "God is love," then the feeling of love brings us closer to God.

These inspirational movies could be of two types: externally or internally focused. For an externally focused inspirational film, think *Erin Brockovich*. Unemployed single mother gets job, discovers that the evil, malevolent power company is poisoning the water supply, and she triumphs over them.

Metaphysical movies, however, are more of the internally focused variety of inspirational films. Although *The Matrix*, for instance, has a lot of action in it, the reason for it being a stand-out (from this book's perspective) is the *internal* transformation Neo undergoes. Mr. Anderson becomes Neo – the One – by learning to believe that he *is* the One. His teachers – notably Morpheus, the Oracle, and even the Spoon Boy – each in his or her own way point back at Neo that it's all on him and his beliefs.

Or take two key, internally focused, transformations in *Inception*. Dom Cobb – while gifted – is highly limited in his ability to function because he is wracked with guilt over the suicide of his wife, Mal. He tortures himself because he believes that his actions drove her to kill herself. It is only when he tells her toward the end of *Inception*, "And now I have to let go," that he can unburden himself, and really get on with the task he has before him, and ultimately his life.

Similarly, in *Inception*, Peter Fischer has labored since childhood under the mistaken notion that his dying father had said he was "disappointed" in his son. This was a kind of master grievance (affecting even his very identity) that had limited him for his entire life. Cobb's team offered him an alternative way of looking at the situation; that Fischer had misheard his father, that he'd been disappointed that the younger Fischer *"had tried"* to emulate the elder Fischer. This goes back to the idea that everything is perception. By looking at a situation in a different way, we find that it can lead to an inner transformation.

The inception team's revisionist history did the trick. They changed Fischer's mind, albeit ultimately through sophisticated manipulation for profit.

The *Big* Questions

In their 2006 book *Spiritual Cinema*, Stephen Simon and Gay Hendricks suggest that there's a newer genre of film that they have titled "Spiritual Cinema." They say that this movie category "tells great stories that ask the big questions about life and living: Who are we? Where do we come from? Where are we going? And what can we become when we're at our best?"

The authors contrast "Spiritual Cinema" with "Religious Cinema," in that "Spiritual Cinema does not provide dogmatic answers to the aforementioned questions – rather it inspires you to come up with your own answers." (To avoid this confusion, this book prefers the term "metaphysical." It covers similar territory as Simon and Hendricks's book, but it dives more deeply into the deconstruction of each film.)

Of course, some films can fit into both genres. While it is not contained in this book, a future volume in this series of *Reel Vision* will include *Brother Sun, Sister Moon*. This biopic about St. Francis of Assisi is clearly about a religious icon, but also is the portrayal of a radical thinker who asked big questions and lived his creed in a profoundly inspirational manner.

In the Foreword, I have described how this book came about. In a sense, it amounts to me finding my own answers. But I don't kid myself. This is not so much a book of answers to life's mysteries, but rather a book about films that *ask provocative questions*. It would be nice and tidy if "the Truth" was a simple matter easily explained. Nice but, I'd submit, not the case.

On the other hand, the Truth is true. The alternative would get us all a one-way ticket to the asylum!

So, think of it this way for a moment:

1) There is Truth. It is true.

2) Virtually all of humanity through the millennia have failed at finding pure, abiding Truth.

3) Probably most of us have gotten pretty good, though, at identifying *un*truths. We encounter untruths virtually every day of our conscious lives. Separating the wheat from the chaff is our full-time job.

4) One's ability to perceive, intuit, and think makes one better at more consistently identifying, and rejecting, untruths. This requires an inquisitive and determined mind, which are themselves learned habits.

5) Those abilities can be fostered by exposing ourselves to a variety of philosophies, people, and art forms. We can try them on, feel our way around, test, and play with ideas and emotions to determine if they work for us. For many, a certain philosophy-of-life will work for us for a while, only to be discarded when it stops working.

6) Often, the ups and downs of life will lead to a *big* down, a "dark night of the soul." Some never recover from these. Others find these sorts of tests to be their greatest life lessons.

7) But, make no mistake, we are virtually all stumbling our way through life. Some may do so more gracefully than others. Some recover quickly from setbacks. Fully enlightened beings, however, are the rarest of birds. Odds are extremely long that people who *claim* to know the Truth are confused, lying, delusional, or outright daft. Few – make that almost none – know Truth with a capital T.

8) We all, on the other hand, get *glimpses* of Truth, those moments of clarity when there are no questions and all is right with the world and with ourselves.

9) With help and determination, we can have these moments more frequently.

Which brings us back to film, especially what I am calling "metaphysical cinema." The five films contained in this first volume (*The Matrix, Dark City, Inception, Revolver,* and *Vanilla Sky*) are each films that can be profoundly helpful pointing us toward Truth and away from untruth. It's also highly likely that, in watching each of these films just once as mere entertainment, most would miss just how deep these films are.

Metaphysical Thought Experiments
Exposing ourselves to the ideas contained in these metaphysical movies can be helpful in a variety of ways. We may find these films entertaining and stimulating. It opens us up to possibilities by taking us to different places, emotionally and intellectually. Rather than experimenting with different ways of being in the world, we can watch others do it on the screen, and let it play out in our minds.

Imagine what it might be like to be David Aames in *Vanilla Sky*. Everything that seems to happen to him has *not* happened. Instead, he's been cryogenically preserved, and his dreams in that state have turned to nightmares. With that as a premise, then consider the possibility that the life you are leading right now, and your history, is all *false!* If you knew that – really knew it – it seems unlikely that you would fret about the things you fret about. By the same token, the things that give you a rush might not provoke such ecstatic states. Life would not feel so much like a rollercoaster ride anymore.

Others might have a different reaction. As Aames's sidekick Brian says to him, "…but one day you'll know what love truly is. It's the sour and the sweet. And I know sour which allows me to appreciate the sweet." Perhaps you really *like* the peaks and valleys of life, so rather than smooth out the ride, you'll revel in both the highs and the lows. You will come to more fully appreciate *both* the sweet and the sour.

Or consider the case of John Murdoch in *Dark City*. The man is highly disoriented during much of the film. It's as if he has a profound case of amnesia, as he doesn't even know his name at the film's opening. Nothing in the world makes any sense to him. While a very extreme case, haven't we all had our days when not much of anything makes much, or even any, sense?

And talk about the-agony-and-the-ecstasy-filled life that Jake Green leads in *Revolver*. Jake's rollercoaster life has him down while in jail; then he gets out, rising to amass a fortune; down again when his boss puts a hit out on him and is diagnosed with a fatal illness; but then rises like a phoenix out of the ashes as he comes out at the other end the better man for all of his trials by fire.

Love's Labor's Lost, and Found

These movies didn't just happen. They each took years to write, develop, and produce by the creative teams that made them. It was no accident that the Wachowskis offered us a lesson in epistemology when they put on the screen the white-room, Construct sequence in the *The Matrix*.

The Wachowskis – the sibling co-writers/directors – had something to say, but they said it subtly, through allegory, with deep philosophical concepts that are seamlessly woven into the fabric of an entertainment medium. The film easily could just have been a sci-fi/action movie, and likely could have had just as much box-office appeal as *The Matrix* as-produced did. *Sans* the philosophical messages contained in *The Matrix*, it may have still been a commercial success, but its impact on the culture would likely have been fleeting.

The thought-provoking aspect of *The Matrix* may have made it *more* commercial. This cannot be proven, but recall that this book's premise is that we are all philosophers, in a sense. Even those who watch a movie "to escape" are committing a philosophical act!

A person making the choice to seek "escape" has decided that he or she needs something to escape *from*. "Something is wrong with the state of my mind," the escape seeker implicitly is saying to him- or herself, "I want to see an escapist film to take my mind off my troubles."

This is a philosophical stance, even if we don't label it "philosophy." A choice is being made. Some may claim, "I just like action movies, and I like to watch them on a big screen in a darkened theater. There's nothing more to it."

They are not really paying attention to their headspace by making such a claim. Thoughts and emotions are working below the surface for such a person. Movies remind us of conscious or subconscious memories, and therefore involve thought and choice, which necessarily involve a form of philosophizing, albeit not "sophisticated" academic-style inquiry.

Based on their work, the Wachowskis are two quite radical thinkers. They are also gifted filmmakers. The impact of film is arguably a more effective means to share their radical ideas that is akin to a Trojan Horse, where the outer package is different than the philosophy that is wrapped up within it.

Whether the Wachowskis view themselves as philosophers is hard to say. Most filmmakers think of themselves as entertainers first and foremost; some might say they are artists, or storytellers. Few would say they are philosophers, but this book's contention is that we are *necessarily all* philosophers. In the case of the Wachowskis and the other filmmakers of the flicks in this book, these entertainer/artist/storytellers happen to have a very strong point-of-view in their work. And that point-of-view shines through in these works identified here as the great metaphysical movies.

Christopher Nolan made *Inception* between the second and third installments of the *Dark Knight* trilogy, runaway box office hits all. Nolan is what's known in Hollywood as "bankable"; giving him $160 million to make a film that must have sounded "way out there" by the studio executives was a risk they were willing to take because he is *Christopher Nolan*.

It seems likely that Nolan could easily continue to make more conventional, commercial, blockbuster-type movies, ones more likely to reap more profits for himself and the studios. But, as can be seen in Nolan's earlier work, *Memento*, the *auteur* clearly has something to say in his film work beyond just making money. Nolan plays with what might happen to someone who loses his ability to remember anything after a certain traumatic event, in this case, his wife being killed by attackers. *Memento* clearly demonstrates that the man is metaphysically inclined – deeply so, in fact.

"My Brain is Only a Receiver..."

It's been said that genius often requires some form of inspiration. This applies not only to filmmaking, but other sophisticated endeavors as well, from music composition to engineering. Nikola Tesla – considered by many as the greatest inventor of the 20th century – would identify a problem in existing technology, let it simmer in his mind for a time, and then the solution or invention would just pop into his mind nearly fully formed. "My brain is only a receiver. In the Universe there is a core from which we obtain knowledge, strength, and inspiration," Tesla once said.

Imagine if Tesla's idea is roughly correct, then we can infer that we are receivers of a sort. Some may be more open to the "signals" than others. Each person's capabilities would just manifest differently. So, Tesla "received" alternating current electricity and fluorescent light bulbs. Guy Ritchie "received" *Revolver*. And so on.

This is not to say that great accomplishment does not require some determined work. But there does seem to be an element of "something else" inspiring the geniuses whose impressive achievements enrich our lives.

Many films since the commercial art form began in the early 20th century certainly contain metaphysical and psycho-spiritual themes. The 1939 version of *The Wizard of Oz* (a silent version was made in 1925), while on the surface a children's film, is deeply metaphysical. Many sci-fi and fantasy films through the decades have touched on metaphysical themes.

Dreaming: The Universal Experience

All the films in this first volume occur in one way or another in a dreamscape, i.e., in the mind of the characters. So much can and has been said about dreams and dreaming, but for purposes of this book, what seems most germane is that dreams involve the creation of worlds where anything is possible. Unburdened by heavy realities, a dreamer can and does either create his or her own world, or re-arrange his or her memories from waking-state experiences. One could say that movies are what dreams are made of, since one's imagination can paint anything on the canvas of film.

While humans have dreamed dreams throughout history, even those who study dreams ("oneirology" is the name of the field) still don't know why we dream at night. The Greeks and Romans thought that dreams were messages from the Gods. This concept was echoed by Tesla: We are *receivers*.

The lyric, "Lose your dreams and you will lose your mind," contains much truth. Although the Rolling Stones when they produced *Ruby Tuesday* were likely referring to visualizing goals in life, this is still in accord with what many sleep scientists believe. Dreaming contributes mightily to a person's cognitive and emotional health. Sleep (and dream) deprivation can lead to serious neurological impairment.

Wherever our dreams come from, dreaming seems to be as universal an experience as breathing and eating. Yet, because dreams are usually about different subjects, tailored to the individual, we could say that we are all "filmmakers," each producing our own "film project" spontaneously, up to seven times a night.

The influence of the 20th century psychiatrists Sigmund Freud and (possibly more so) Carl Jung on dream interpretation and dream theory are great influences on these metaphysically themed films. This is not to assert that, say, Christopher Nolan has necessarily read Freud or Jung, but that their influence on the world's knowledge base has seeped into many aspects of the culture.

On the other hand, it seems all-but-certain that the Wachowskis, Alex Proyas, Christopher Nolan, Guy Ritchie, and Cameron Crowe have all read some Joseph Campbell, who was greatly influenced by Jung. His writings on archetypes and myths is widely read and used in the creative community. You could say that Campbell and his hero myths are *de rigeur* in Hollywood.

So, the ripe field for the metaphysical movie was seeded by European psychologists whose ideas spread like wildfire in America and beyond. However, the other major stream that underlies these metaphysical movies is Eastern spirituality.

Up the Yin Yang

Interestingly, Campbell at the age of 20 – while traveling with his family on an ocean-liner back to the U.S. from a trip to Europe – happened to meet J. Krishnamurti, also a young man at the time. Born in India, Krishnamurti went on to become one of the most influential teachers of Eastern spirituality in the Western world. This chance encounter was fortuitous and pivotal in shifting Campbell's thinking.

Campbell was fascinated by Krishnamurti's ideas, and went on to study Sanskrit and the Hindu text, *Upanishads*. Campbell's oft-repeated mantra, "Follow your bliss" and the philosophy around that concept is heavily influenced by the *Upanishads*.

Jung himself was deeply influenced by *Bardo Thodol* (also known as *The Tibetan Book of the Dead*). The Swiss psychiatrist resonated with Buddhism and the spiritual insights from Tibet.[5]

It's above the pay grade of this book to speculate and trace movements of thought to explain why there's been such a surge of metaphysical movies in recent years. It's safe to say that the confluence of the psychology of dreams and Eastern spirituality would seem to be at least major contributing factors to the metaphysical movie movement.

God Incarnate

In a movie that will be in a future volume in this series, *Waking Life*, filmmaker Caveh Zahedi offers his take on the spiritual implications of film. As he paraphrases André Bazin, a film critic and theorist, Zahedi gives us a glimpse into the deeper meaning that films capture.

> "... and so what film is actually capturing is like God incarnate, creating. And this very moment, God is manifesting as this. And what the film would capture if it was filming us right now would be like God as this table, and God as you, and God as me, and God looking the way we look right now, and saying and thinking what we're thinking right now, because we are all God manifest in that sense. So film is actually like a record of God, or of the face of God, or of the ever-changing face of God."

He goes on:

> "And that's what film has. It's just that moment, which is holy. You know, like this moment, it's holy. But we walk around like it's not holy. We walk around like there's some holy moments and there are all the other moments that are not holy, right, but this moment is holy, right? And if film can let us see that, like frame it so that we see, like, 'Ah, this moment. Holy.' And it's like 'Holy, holy, holy' moment by moment."

I would have to agree with Zahedi and Bazin, at least in my experience. Having watched these metaphysical movies as closely as I do, I sometimes find that these sorts of films are a powerful form of meditation. Unlike, say, breath work or mindfulness meditation, watching a film can take us to "another place" in our heads. Watching it again, and again, we begin to understand the film at deeper and deeper levels. In so doing, profound insights can be unlocked or enhanced.

For example, I believe I understand psychological projection better now having watched and absorbed *Inception*. I understood projection well from an *intellectual* perspective prior to seeing the film, but *Inception* provided me with an *emotional* understanding that I didn't have previously.

David Hoffmeister, author of *The Movie Watcher's Guide to Enlightenment*, has described this active-watching of these sorts of films – sometimes multiple times – as "mind rinses." With our active ego mind quelled while watching a flick, metaphysical movies can teach us important lessons as they sink into our consciousness, repairing us both emotionally and intellectually.

All in all, how it works seems beside the point. As you read the deconstructed movies in this volume and watch the movies with some new insights, the greatest (and only) measure of their validity is *how it makes you feel*. Has it added to your understanding in some way, or enhanced your view of the world in a positive manner? If so, my job is complete.

OK, the stage is set.

Now, on with the show!

Endnotes for Introduction

[1.] "Attendance history - World cinema stats," Screenville (2011), screenville.blogspot.com/2011/09/attendance-history-world-cinema-stats.html

[2.] Paul Bond, "Study: Global Entertainment Industry Poised to Top $2 Trillion in 2016," The Hollywood Reporter, (2013), www.billboard.com/biz/articles/news/global/1565728/study-global-entertainment-industry-poised-to-top-2-trillion-in

[3.] PricewaterhouseCoopers, "Global Entertainment and Media Outlook, 2014-2018," (2013), http://www.pwc.com/gx/en/global-entertainment- media-outlook/segment-insights/filmed-entertainment.jhtml

[4.] Wikipedia (2014), "List of countries by GDP (nominal)," en.wikipedia.org/wiki/List_of_countries_by_GDP_(nominal)

[5.] Jung has been quoted as saying of *Bardo Thodol*: "[It] belongs to that class of writings which not only are of interest to specialists in Mahayana Buddhism, but also, because of their deep humanity and still deeper insight into the secrets of the human psyche, make an especial appeal to the layman seeking to broaden his knowledge of life... For years, ever since it was first published, the *Bardo Thodol* has been my constant companion, and to it I owe not only many stimulating ideas and discoveries, but also many fundamental insights."

The Matrix: Reality is a thing of the past

Released in 1999, *The Matrix* is perhaps *the* standard-bearer for the metaphysical film. Not only is *The Matrix* shot through with allegorical content, but it's a film that works on a lot of levels for a wide range of audiences. Science fiction and/or fantasy films lend themselves to thinking about the world from a higher vantage point, as stepping out of the mire of everyday life allows us to see philosophical and spiritual matters without the prejudices we might bring to a more pedestrian film about, say, cops and robbers.

By the late 90s when *The Matrix* was released, the computer age was fully embedded in the common culture. Unlike in the 1960s when the culture's perception of computers was mostly a matter of science fiction like *Star Trek*, by 1999 most people in Western society had at least used a computer at work and roughly half of all households owned one. It is interesting to note as well that, at root, computer software is binary – everything comes down to a 1 or a 0. So does spirituality, i.e., true/false; Heaven/Hell; God/man; right/wrong. It becomes fitting that the Wachowskis (Andy and now Lana, the co-writers/directors of *The Matrix*) chose to begin the film with a blinking cursor on a black computer screen.

At first viewing, we can't really know what the voice-over conversation between Cypher and Trinity – two important characters in this filmic saga – is all about. We only get the sense that someone is being observed. But, by doing so, the Wachowskis capture our interest from the outset of this seminal film. They open up our minds to the possibilities of alternate universes and non-dualistic thinking.

Who is "The One"?
The voice of Cypher is the voice for skepticism. Consider this quick back and forth, done in voice-overs:

TRINITY: Morpheus believes he is the One.

CYPHER: Do you?

TRINITY: I...it doesn't matter what I believe.

CYPHER: You don't, do you?

A key theme throughout *The Matrix* involves the extent to which the characters have unconflicted, true faith. And the "faith" involves, ultimately, a faith in *oneself*, the individual's ability to discern truth from untruth. This ability to choose against the false throughout the film comes down to an *emotional knowing*, versus a rote acceptance of what an authority figure asserts the truth to be.

One of the reasons that *The Matrix* was such a sensation is that it is heavily punctuated with action. Early on, we meet Trinity (played by Carrie-Anne Moss) clad in a black PVC outfit. Her impossible Kung Fu moves further draw us into the film, while we still don't know who she is, or what she's up to. We want to *know*!

Revenge of the Nerds

The intrigue turns inward from action to the cerebral, as we meet Neo (played by Keanu Reeves). An earlier draft of the screenplay describes him as "a younger man who knows more about living inside a computer than living outside one."

In some ways, the casting of Reeves as a computer geek seems a bit off because of his striking features. (Reeves's heritage – including English, Native Hawaiian, Chinese, Irish, and Portuguese ancestry – gives him an uncommon look, clearly not your stereotypical geek.) The Wachowskis have been quoted as saying of the Reeves casting: "Keanu has a boyish quality about him that was perfect for the role, but at the same time he has a maturity that allows his character to develop and eventually take control of the situation."[1]

This geek known as Thomas Anderson, or "Mr. Anderson" as he comes to be mockingly called by the agents, needs to become a super-hero, so Reeves seems to have been an ideal casting decision for a role that's become iconic.

Even the name "Thomas Anderson" could very well have been chosen as a hidden message in *The Matrix*. In Greek, Ander or Andreas means "man." Ander-son would mean "Son of Man," a term used to describe Jesus.

And the name Thomas could well be a nod to the Apostle Thomas, who is known to most Christians as Doubting Thomas. As we shall see, the name choice of Thomas for Neo by the Wachowskis is very apropos. In recent decades there has been increased interest in the Apostle Thomas, since the findings of additional Gospels in Nag Hammadi, Egypt. The Gospel of Thomas has become one of the more notable ones, painting Jesus' teachings with a more Gnostic flavor.

Waking Up Is Hard To Do

In the beginning of the movie, as Neo intensely probes the 'Net, he has his own "ah-ha moment." He's just about to disconnect from his computer, when across the screen the words flash:

"Wake up, Neo."

Next, the words scroll by on the screen:

"The Matrix has you."

And then:

"Follow the white rabbit."

And then finally it reads:

"Knock, knock, Neo."

As this occurs, we hear a knock on Neo's door, which startles him.

We learn that the person knocking on the door is his acquaintance, Choi, accompanied by DuJour. The timing seems to be purely coincidental, but Choi and Anderson had clearly previously discussed meeting up for this business transaction.

Choi gives Neo "two grand" and in return, Neo gives him a computer disk. It is of note that Neo pulls the disk out of a hollowed-out book titled: *Simulacra and Simulations*.

Simulacra and Simulations was published in 1981 by French academic Jean Baudrillard, who offers a challenging take on every day (what we call) "reality." "Reality," according to Baudrillard, has been replaced with *symbols* of reality in modern society – they could even be called simulations. As we shall see, it's no coincidence that *The Matrix* is rife with symbols and simulations.

Many commenters have noted that the Wachowskis have had several philosophical influences woven throughout their movies: Plato, especially the Cave allegory *(See Appendix A for more on Plato's Cave)*; the epistemology of Descartes; Socrates and his storied visit to the Oracle of Delphi; Gnostic Christianity; Buddhism; Werner Erhard and the Landmark Forum; and of course Baudrillard.

The Unsuspecting Savior
Upon Neo giving Choi the expensive computer disk, he expresses his gratitude, as he tells Neo: "Hallelujah! You are my Savior, man! My own personal Jesus."

Like a fisherman tugging a fish in, the Wachowskis are gradually establishing that Neo is "special," a messiah of some sort. There has already been some talk about the One. The name "Neo" is an anagram for "One," and now we have Choi likening Neo to Jesus.

Neo seems a bit pasty and out-of-sorts to Choi. At first he refers obliquely to his computer, but then Neo confesses: "You ever have the feeling that you're not sure if you're awake or still dreaming?"

This idea of the material world being a dreamstate touches upon Eastern spiritual philosophy, particularly Buddhism and Hinduism, and has been used in much metaphysical cinema. The notion of "Maya" undergirds those religious traditions, suggesting that the material world is a vast illusion. We also see this idea in Western spiritual thought, such as in *A Course in Miracles* (ACIM).

The Judeo-Christian Bible has some verses that point to the state of dreaming. The Bible states: "So the Lord God caused the man (Adam) to fall into a deep sleep; and while he was sleeping, he took one of the man's ribs and closed up the place with flesh." (Gen. 2:21, KJV [King James Version]) Note that nowhere does it say that Adam ever *woke*. We could easily infer that the material world is a dream, some might say a long nightmare.

Sign, Sign, Everywhere a Sign

Choi and DuJour attempt to convince Neo to come to a party with them. Neo doesn't seem interested at first, being rather distracted by the messages coming across his computer, but then he notices that DuJour has a *white rabbit* tattooed on her shoulder.

A sign if ever there was one!

Jolted by this "white rabbit" appearance, Neo decides to go out with Choi and DuJour to "follow the white rabbit." As if on cue, when they arrive at their destination, Trinity appears. No shrinking violet she, Trinity approaches Neo. She tells him, "I know a lot about you. I've been wanting to meet you for some time."

He finds out that Trinity had sent the note about the Matrix and the white rabbit. She not only has been watching Neo, but is concerned that "they" are, too. She tells him, "...you are in danger. I brought you here to warn you." Who "they" are and what "they" want, Trinity won't say, but this intrigue keeps us *very* interested.

She continues: "I know why you're here, Neo. I know what you've been doing. I know why you hardly sleep, why you live alone and why, night after night, you sit at your computer. You're looking for him. I know because I was once looking for the same thing, but when he found me he told me I wasn't really looking for him. I was looking for an answer."

Trinity is describing something tantamount to a burning spiritual seeking.

"What Is The Matrix?"

She goes on: "It's the question that drives us, the question that brought you here. You know the question just as I did."

Neo responds with the simple question: "What is the Matrix?"

Recounting her sage's advice, Trinity says: "When I asked him, he said that no one could ever be told the answer to that question. They have to see it to believe it. The answer is out there, Neo. It's looking for you and it will find you, if you want it to."

"Seek, and ye shall find," seems an almost trite statement when applied in this instance, and yet *The Matrix* shows us a personal path to salvation, in this case for Mr. Thomas Anderson, a.k.a., Neo.

Salvation may be something that can be found by reading scripture, attending church, and doing good works. However, the Wachowskis seem to suggest that salvation is an individualized matter. No one can *give* you salvation. You must go out (or, that is, go *in* through contemplation and inquiry) and actively seek it.

Take This Job...

This evening was quite the turning point for Neo. However, his day-to-day life situation remains the same, and upon rising the next morning he finds that he is already late for work.

The next scene has Neo at work being castigated by his boss: "You have a problem with authority, Mr. Anderson. You believe that you are special, that somehow the rules do not apply to you. Obviously, you are mistaken."

While this dressing-down is occurring, two window washers are outside on scaffolding, their squeegees cleaning the skyscraper's windows. This is a foreshadowing, as Neo is about to have his old life stripped away.

Mr. Anderson returns to his cubicle where he receives a mysterious package containing a cell phone. Immediately upon opening it, the cell phone rings. It's Morpheus with an urgent message: "They're coming for you, Neo."

Like the Holy Spirit providing worldly guidance, Morpheus gives Neo instructions to escape from the agents, with the caveat that Neo must do *exactly* as he says.

Despite the fact that Morpheus is in a remote location, he somehow flawlessly guides Neo. However, Morpheus wants him to take a trusting leap of faith and walk out onto a high-rise ledge. These mysteries add to the allure of the movie as we wonder, "How on Earth is this escape going to work?"

I Fought the Law, and the Law Won

Neo disregards Morpheus's last death-defying instruction, and is apprehended. He's handcuffed and driven off by the agents, and finds himself seated in an interrogation room. Agent Smith comes in with a thick file and accuses Neo (a.k.a., Mr. Anderson) of violating practically every computer crime imaginable, and even worse, being in league with

Morpheus, the most notorious terrorist on Earth. Agent Smith offers leniency if Neo will agree to cooperate with the agency to bring Morpheus to justice.

Again, Neo demonstrates that he does indeed have a problem with authority. To Agent Smith's offer, Neo responds by giving him the finger and demanding his phone call.

Here things take a turn for the weird. Somehow Agent Smith plays with the laws of physics and seals Neo's mouth so he can no longer speak. The Agents restrain him, and then insert into Neo's abdomen an electronic device that becomes some kind of animated insect.

We cut quickly to Neo's bedroom, where he awakens, screaming. He examines his mouth and stomach, attempting to determine whether the interrogation by Agent Smith actually happened or instead was a nightmare. This gives us a glimpse into the illusory power of the Matrix. The laws that we believe are infallible (gravity, for instance) are manipulated, by who or what is still unclear. We are given the impression from this scene (and more to come) that the laws of nature aren't laws at all, but instead are mere tendencies.

Meeting Morpheus

As if on cue, Neo's phone rings. It's Morpheus, who then proceeds to tell Neo that he's "the One," and offering that he's been searching for Neo his whole life. Heady but unconventional stuff! Neo agrees to meet Morpheus.

A car with Trinity and two others pull over to pick Neo up. Despite the fact that we're led to believe that Morpheus and his associates are on Neo's side, they point a gun at him, as well as a strange steel-and-glass device. They demand that he take off his shirt.

Again confronted with a hostile authority figure, Neo resists. Rather than be reasonable, Switch (played by Belinda McClory) says assertively: "Right now there is only one rule. Our way or the highway." Neo's "trust issues" are being tested once again early in *The Matrix*.

Given that they already know one another, Trinity intervenes. "Neo, please, you have to trust me," she says.

Logically, Neo responds: "Why?"

To which she replies, "Because you've been down there, Neo. You already know that road. You know exactly where it ends."

To be sure, Neo has been searching for something. By all indications, his life has taken a turn for the worse. Authority figures from all sides are threatening him, interrogating him, and otherwise making his life a living hell. He decides to trust Trinity and, by extension, Morpheus.

And in this case, these associates of Morpheus's have benign intent. The steel-and-glass device is used to remove the "bug" that Agent Smith did indeed insert into Mr. Anderson. It was no dream.

The Wachowskis are amping up the questions, what is real and what is a dream? Mr. Anderson is, in a sense, having his apple-cart of a life up-ended. Something about his "reality" is, at the very least, suspect.

Now debugged, this foursome arrive at Morpheus's headquarters where Neo finally meets the mystery man himself. Neo and Morpheus (played by Laurence Fishburne) sit for what is to be one of the classic first encounters in film ever.

...Like A Splinter In Your Mind...

After some brief chit chat, Morpheus states: "I imagine, right now, you must be feeling a bit like Alice, tumbling down the rabbit hole?" Offering this allusion of one of the seminal fantasies in literature (*Alice in Wonderland*) is no mistake, for *The Matrix* is about to shift from the real to the surreal.

It's been said that there is only one truth, although there are many paths to it. It – truth – will not only set you free, but can be read two ways: first, by seeking and embracing the truth, one will be unburdened in some form. However, it can also be read as a prediction. You *will* be set free...eventually.

Morpheus now has Neo's, and our, full attention. He continues: "Unfortunately, no one can be told what the Matrix is. You have to see it for yourself."

Red Pill or Blue?

This transitions into one of the most profound moments in film history. Morpheus offers Neo in either hand a red and a blue pill.

"You take the blue pill and the story ends," Morpheus says. "You wake in your bed and you believe whatever you want to believe. You take the red pill and you stay in Wonderland and I show you how deep the rabbit-hole goes."

It seems hardly a choice in the moment, and of course Neo takes the red pill. But, just to be certain, Morpheus concludes: "Remember that all I am offering is the truth. Nothing more." A bold move on Neo's part, almost begging us to wonder whether we would be so fearless in a similar circumstance.

In some ways, this sequence has an electric kool-aid feel to it, with Morpheus playing Ken Kesey. (Kesey is perhaps best known as the author of *One Flew Over the Cuckoo's Nest* and an impresario of LSD parties that were chronicled in Tom Wolfe's 1968 classic *The Electric Kool-Aid Acid Test*.) Neo is led to a kind of examination room, where

Morpheus obliquely explains that his red pill is part of a "trace program," one that will help Morpheus "pinpoint" Neo's location. Not surprisingly this confuses Neo, who asks, "What does that mean?"

One of Morpheus's associates, Cypher (played by Joe Pantoliano), interjects: "It means buckle up, Dorothy, 'cause Kansas is going bye-bye."

At this point, Neo is no doubt about as psychologically off-balance as he can be. But Morpheus keeps pushing him: "Have you ever had a dream, Neo, that you were so sure was real?"

Morpheus piles on: "What if you were unable to wake from that dream, Neo? How would you know the difference between the dreamworld and the real world?" We can easily put ourselves in Neo's shoes here and question what we ourselves call "reality."

The red pill starts to kick in now. A kind of gel crawls up Neo's arms. Not surprisingly, he finds this "dream" to be more like a "nightmare." But things get weirder still. Neo seems to be sucked out of this room and into a magenta gelatin vat. His body is covered with metal, umbilical-cord-like tubes.

After panicky struggle, a bald, naked Neo emerges from this gelatinous goo. As the camera pulls back, we see that Neo is in a pod-like structure. His is one of thousands of pods. This set has an eerie, dystopian feel to it.

Suddenly, an insect-like flying machine swoops into Neo's airspace. After menacingly hovering over him, the machine seizes Neo. He's paralyzed as the machine injects something into the person formerly known as Mr. Anderson.

After the needle is pulled out, Neo is pulled into a kind of waterpark ride filled with a gelatin sludge. It's as if Neo is a newborn, who has just emerged from the birth canal. Neo begins to drown, but is snatched out of this waste-water nightmare by a futuristic hovercraft. In the hold, Neo meets up again with Morpheus.

Welcome to the Real World
"Welcome to the real world, Neo," Morpheus says with a certain poignancy. The screen fades to black, amping up the drama of what's transpired.

Having gone deeply into the rabbit hole and now returned to Morpheus and the crew, we learn that his muscles are atrophied. He looks like a human pin cushion, as he receives some unconventional medical treatment.

Neo asks, "Why do my eyes hurt?"

Morpheus responds pregnantly, "You've never used them before."

In other words, as it says in the New Testament, Neo was blind, but now he can see.

Morpheus, having put Neo through the ringer, now takes a more gentle approach with his newfound protégé. He reveals to Neo where they are and what this "real world" is all about. For instance, it's not 1997, but 2197. They are aboard a ship named the Nebuchadnezzar.

Sand or Rock?

Again, the Wachowskis take a metaphysical turn. In the Bible, Nebuchadnezzar was a king of Babylon, one who searched for meaning in his dreams. The story of Nebuchadnezzar is – among other things – a cautionary tale, as Nebuchadnezzar was filled with pride. This pride led Daniel, who became Nebuchadnezzar's advisor and dream interpreter, to suggest that the king had "feet of clay." In other words, Nebuchadnezzar's foundation – his core principles – was weak.

This one's a two-fer by the Wachowskis. The Biblical Nebuchadnezzar wanted to understand his dreams, as does Thomas Anderson/Neo. His "dreams" included his searching the Internet for Morpheus and for meaning in his "in-the-Matrix" life. Something wasn't adding up, but he could not identify what the splinter in his mind was all about.

More deeply, Neo was looking in the wrong place with the wrong tools. He'd been effectively hypnotized by the Matrix, believing that the life he was living was a real one. As we are finding out now, Neo was living a dream. Like the Biblical Nebuchadnezzar's feet of clay, Neo's foundation – his belief system – was flawed, deeply so.

As Jesus' suggestion to Peter to build a foundation on rock, not sand, Daniel was essentially exhorting King Nebuchadnezzar to tend to his "foundation," or, in a sense, his core principles.

Up to this point, much of *The Matrix* is about Neo discovering that his core thought system is not working. Why not? They don't work because they are based on false premises. We shall see that by him taking the red pill of truth, his very foundation and fundamental beliefs are going to be challenged and replaced.

After touring the ship and meeting the rest of the crew, Morpheus turns to Neo and says: "You want to know what the Matrix is, Neo? The answer is right here," as he touches the back of Neo's head. This is not only a physical pointing but a metaphysical one as well. Morpheus indicates that the Matrix takes place in the mind.

Then, they literally plug a coaxial cable into Neo's head, where he and the rest of the crew have permanent jacks.

Residual Self-Image

This leads to the next scene, perhaps that most pedagogic of the film. By plugging into the Matrix, Neo and Morpheus are transported to "the Construct." Morpheus explains that in this "loading program," things can be materialized in one's mind.

In the Construct, we are told that a person will appear as a "residual self-image. The mental projection of your electronic self." These residual self-images are the Wachowskis's way of explaining "psychological projection," a concept first attributed to Freud. Humans have a marked tendency to define themselves by what they see in the world around them. Everything that we see – we label, categorize, and build a story about its meaning. Importantly, our self-image is how we fit into this projection.

What Morpheus is doing is explaining to Neo that these projected stories are our own inventions. The world – and we as individuals – is neutral; it has no meaning, it just is. The mind ascribes meaning to the wholly neutral physical universe.

Consider an extreme example. Anorexics often see themselves as "fat" even though they are skin and bones. We're all doing this – telling distorted stories about the world and ourselves to some extent. This is our residual self-image.

Neo touches things in the Construct, and as far as he's concerned, they are "real." His senses tell him that his eyes see images, his ears hear sounds, his fingers feel objects, and yet, it all happens while he is sitting in a chair plugged into the Construct.

To put a point on this learning experience for Neo, Morpheus asks a very pertinent question: "What is real? How do you define real? If you're talking about what you feel, taste, smell, or see, then real is simply electrical signals interpreted by your brain."

If there was any question that the Wachowskis have done some deep spiritual and epistemic work, this dialog should erase those doubts. How indeed do we define real? Throughout our lives we proceed with the assumption that, for example, seeing is believing. But few stop to ask: What is seeing? And what makes us believe what we see is really there?

Morpheus answers the question most forthrightly...seeing is "simply electrical signals interpreted by your brain." We may believe that our eyes see or our ears hear but, according to Morpheus, we are incorrect. *(For a deeper dive into this part of the film, see Appendix B: Further Reflections on* The Matrix.*)*

We may insist and believe wholeheartedly that we are looking, hearing, and seeing reality, for we have always trusted our senses, but in actuality, we can't really be sure that it is true.

As the filmic experience of *The Matrix* whooshes by us, the Wachowskis drop a lot of bread crumbs. This is a movie, however, and movies need to keep moving. There's no time to pause and ponder. But, because our emotions are up and our defenses are down, *The Matrix* is teaching us by touching us subconsciously.

Some might call this "benign brainwashing"!

The point is that Morpheus is challenging Neo's thought system down to the core by questioning the very reality that Thomas Anderson thought to be "the truth." By doing so, Neo's slate is being wiped clean and his mind can, in effect, be rewired, preparing him to be the One.

A Trip Down Memory Lane

Morpheus takes Neo on a kind of virtual tour of his late-20th century "world." Showing Neo his physical environment, Morpheus explains: "You have been living inside a dreamworld, Neo." (While it did not make the final cut, the script had this additional dialog: "As in Baudrillard's vision, your whole life has been spent inside the map, not the territory.")

What we can infer from Morpheus's words is that what we perceive as "reality" is, in short, a *virtual* reality. This virtual reality is *not* the real thing, for what one calls "reality" is only what one *believes* is real. There is a difference between perception/belief and truth/reality, for truth is a *constant* no matter what we believe. However, truth is *relative* for the perceiver, that is, different perceivers have different perspectives on what truth is – wars have been fought over these things, for Heaven's sake!

After showing Neo what Earth had really become, Morpheus summarizes: "What is the Matrix? Control." He goes on to explain that the Matrix is a computer-generated dreamworld built to keep us passive and sedated, allowing the artificial-intelligence (AI) machines to use human's energy as a power source.

In a sense, this sheds a new light on Neo's issue with authorities. Prior to meeting Morpheus, Neo was rebelling against social conformity. Now his issues have been bumped up to a new level. These authorities (the AI machines) have manipulated him (and the human race) with authority figures (such as his boss) to keep everyone passive and distracted, all to use them as unwitting energy sources. Now that he has been exposed to the truth of this grand deception, it gives him clarity as to where he should focus his energies so that he can overcome this real threat.

Neo as the Second Coming

Morpheus summarizes the context of the situation by recounting the tale of a man born within the Matrix who had "freed the first of us and taught us the truth; that as long as the Matrix exists, the human race will never be free."

Plainly, what Morpheus is describing is a messiah. He tells Neo that according to the Oracle's prophecy this savior would return, leaving us with the distinct impression that he believes this is who Neo is.

It's interesting to note that the red pill has been chosen by all on board the Nebuchadnezzar, showing that they are all seekers of truth, no longer wanting to live in an illusion. Nevertheless, it seems that even though that this choice was made, it was only a first step. They are still in need of the guidance of a leader, the One, a Messiah.

Jed McKenna, author of *Spiritual Warfare*, contends that while the movie *The Matrix* contains a lot of "useful stuff," it's better to view this tale as "a map on which we can plot our journey, or one leg of it. If the Neo character were really trying to awaken from the dreamstate, he wouldn't have accepted the subterranean world of Morpheus and Zion and the freedom-fighter drama so easily. He'd have recognized it as merely another layer of delusion and kept going."[2]

Many spiritual seekers may find the Wachowskis blatantly Christian allusions over-the-top. It makes Neo special – the One. This could go one of two ways for the metaphysical movie goer; some would welcome a savior or "hero." Or it could make others feel that the rest of us are *less than* the One – unworthy, even. Putting Neo on a Jesus pedestal might imply that we are all sinners who need to beg for forgiveness or require an intermediary to get back to God.

This is a challenge for literature or film in the Joseph Campbell hero's-journey tradition, of which *The Matrix* most assuredly is an example. We get the sense that Neo was effectively born the One, although it's also the case that he has to do his "work," too. He had been a loner/malcontent when we met him, vainly searching the Internet for answers. Neo certainly has a lot of characteristics that we can relate to.

Rather than take issue with the Wachowskis's choice to set Neo up as a messianic hero, it seems just as helpful to simply view him as a leader, a wayshower. In our own lives, doing our own work, we too can be the One. Oneness, after all, sees the world *un*-separated, *un*-splintered.

As discussed in the Introduction, the acclaimed 20th-century inventor Nikola Tesla characterized his mind as a "receiver." Using that analogy as applied to Neo, Morpheus may have seen something about the young man that made him a potentially extraordinary receiver. But, to attain the status of "the One," Neo still needed training to hone his innate abilities.

Let the Games Begin
Neo begins with accelerated computer training in the martial arts. He picks it up extremely quickly. Morpheus enters, suggesting that he and Neo continue to spar in a virtual martial arts studio.

During this encounter, their bodies remain in chairs while their minds share a dream of a martial arts match. Interestingly, their "life systems" are being monitored by a member of the crew. While Morpheus's systems remain stable, Neo's are wild and chaotic. This shows how the virtual Construct is a great classroom for teaching Neo the primacy of the mind, and how to learn to get his emotions under control.

It's been said that the body is, at best, a puppet – a puppet ruled by the mind. As the late Kenneth Wapnick, Ph.D. psychologist and founder of the Foundation for A Course in Miracles, has written:

> "A body doesn't do anything. Can a puppet affect the puppet master? Just think a minute. Can a puppet – except in Twilight Zone – affect a puppet master? Of course not! Anything it does, it does because the puppet master has 'told it to do it'...You pull a string and the mouth moves....The puppet doesn't do that; it's a lifeless piece of wood."[3]

After defeating Neo in the first match, Morpheus asks Neo, "How did I beat you?"

Neo responds, "You – You're too fast."

To which Morpheus replies, "Do you think my being faster, stronger has anything to do with my muscles in this place?"

Since this is a virtual dojo, the answer is, of course, "no." This virtual martial arts contest illustrates for Neo – and for us – that everything is in the mind. Everything.

Lead a Horse to Water
Morpheus continues to challenge Neo, specifically Neo's *mind*. "I'm trying to free your mind, Neo, but all I can do is show you the door," Morpheus implores. "You're the one that has to step through."

Spiritual liberation – at least in the more familiar Christian sense – has two primary models. An aspirant might become devoted to a church's practices while deferring to a hierarchical structure. For example, the Catholic Church has many rules for behavior. These rules are delivered by the clergy and provide Catholics with a specific set of rituals and sacraments that must followed to receive entry into Heaven.

The Protestant Reformation on the other hand was a reaction to this top-down approach, meaning they did not believe in having intermediaries between the parishioners and God thereby having more of a direct contact with God. Martin Luther advocated disintermediating access to the Kingdom. To do so, he translated the Bible into German from Latin to make it more accessible. Generally, it can be said that most mainline Protestant faiths focus less on form, more on content.

Eastern religions have their holy texts as well, but the meditative practices employed by Hindus and Buddhists suggest even more direct communication with a Higher Power. These Eastern religions – generally speaking – focus even less on form, even more on content.

Looking at the training of Neo in the virtual-reality technology of the Construct as a kind of spiritual practice, even these preparations rely on some forms and rituals. But Morpheus as the teacher is consistent. He's interested in the *content* – the result – which is to free Neo's mind.

(An aside: to be clear, this discussion of spiritual approaches is intended for general and illustrative purposes only. There is much wisdom in Mahatma Gandhi's statement: "Truth is one, paths are many.")

In a sense, the "splinter" in Neo's mind – that sense that something is "wrong" with the world – is the part of the mind that is in touch with a Higher Power. The ego – in this case, the ego personality known as Thomas Anderson – is what Morpheus is challenging and ultimately undoing.

Morpheus is playing the part of spiritual drill sergeant. He breaks Neo down through a series of tests, but also builds him up. Morpheus never doubts who Neo really is, and he consistently reinforces the mentor's belief that Neo is the One.

The ego's presence is characterized by suffering, one of the main premises of Buddhism, called "dukkha." Mr. Anderson seemed to suffer greatly, flailing about in his search for truth. Morpheus is helping him to undo his suffering at the source, the mind.

Jump!

For the next phase of training, Morpheus and Neo have the "jump" program fed into their heads. Prior to the challenge of leaping from the roof of one skyscraper to the next, Morpheus says to his trainee: "Let it all go, Neo. Fear. Doubt. Disbelief. Free your mind."

Let us not forget that all of this training is going on in their minds as they sit in a chair plugged into the Construct's illusion of time and space. While there, one is so immersed in what they see, hear, and feel that it is forgotten that they are experiencing a shared dream. Morpheus has a sense of this while Neo is still working on it.

In that dream of time and space, these acts appear to be miraculous, impossible. And yet, it seems that when Morpheus rids himself of these negative thoughts, anything is possible. While Neo has been positioned as "the One," it certainly appears that Morpheus himself has achieved some level of enlightenment. He definitely has taken on the role of Teacher, and looks for his student to surpass him.

In *The Matrix*, we find that Morpheus is teaching Neo that he can perform miracles and defy the laws of nature, too, but that these things are only possible by freeing one's mind. Learning the martial arts was only the first small step in his training.

We would think, for example, that an accelerated martial arts program in the Construct would be different than the impossibility of leaping between (or off of) buildings. Morpheus is showing Neo that miracles are all the same, that there is no order of difficulty between them, for they all take place within a free mind. Again, these seemingly physical acts are taking place as they sit in chairs hooked up to a virtual program.

Erasing *all* doubt is no easy task, even for Neo, the One. He fails in his first attempt to jump over a chasm between buildings. When Morpheus asks him why he failed, Neo responds, "Because...I didn't think I would [make it]?"

Morpheus smiles and nods. His pupil is learning!

To hammer home the power of the mind over matter, when Neo is unplugged, he notices that he's bleeding. "I thought it wasn't real," Neo says to Morpheus.

"Your mind makes it real," his teacher responds.

This is a very important point, showing us the power of belief. Even though Neo is sitting in a chair having a virtual experience, he believes in that (illusory) experience so thoroughly that even though he is not really physically there, he has a physical reaction in the real world *because of* that belief.

Love Your Enemies
In his next lesson in the Construct, Morpheus leads Neo through crowded city streets. He explains: "The Matrix is a system, Neo, and that system is our enemy. But when you are inside and you look around, what do you see? Businessmen, lawyers, teachers, carpenters. The minds of the very people we are trying to save. But until we do, these people are still a part of the system and that makes them our enemy."

31

Morpheus is making an interesting point here in his word choice, one we may have not considered before. How could all of our associates, friends, and even family be called an "enemy"? Calling a "brother" an enemy seems quite incongruous; aren't we supposed to love our neighbor as ourselves?

This message is clear to Morpheus but is new to Neo. The fact is that Neo is still in the process of waking up. He has made the "leap of faith" and taken the red pill, no longer wanting to live in a dream world but in reality. By so doing, as he gets used to this new idea, he is slowly embracing the thought that everything happens in the mind, not in the physical world at all. The *perceived* physical world is the world of the Matrix.

This in itself is a bold path that everybody is not ready to take, and actually engenders fear in many. People will desperately hold onto their version of reality in fear of losing themselves. This will include castigating, deriding, or even killing the person who would contradict them or say something different from what they believe.

There are many parallels to this idea, most notably the crucifixion of Jesus. Others include the allegory of Plato's Cave, where one person saw through the projections on the wall for what they were and walked out into the sunlight. He came back to tell his neighbors of the freedom that was only a few steps away and, for that, they killed him. The truth was too frightening to the many, and fear mobilized them to violence.

Morpheus was helping Neo to *know* the truth himself. Since Neo has made a choice to rise up higher, Morpheus is helping him to be aware not only of the fearful human condition but also to not be dragged back down into the illusion. In this sense, there certainly is no safety in numbers!

From this vantage point far above the maddening crowds, the One is best positioned to save others from their delusions! As Jesus has said in the New Testament; "...Love your enemies, bless them that curse you, do good to them that hate you, and pray for them which despitefully use you, and persecute you." (Matthew 5:44, KJV)

And, then, there is the next piece of dialog from Morpheus that gets to the heart of the matter: "You have to understand that most of these people are not ready to be unplugged and many of them are so inured, so hopelessly dependent on the system that they will fight to protect it."

We're left with the distinct impression that Morpheus also believes that one day they *will* be ready, even though at the present moment they are not.

Fair enough!

Sowing Doubt

After a skirmish with a Sentinel, an attack ship from the "other side," Neo and Cypher share a little downtime. In a moment of candor, Cypher says, "Why, oh why, didn't I take that blue pill?"

Cypher seems to long for that existence. The path he is on now – the hot pursuit of truth – is Spartan and hard, grueling.

Living lives of quiet desperation is, in a sense, familiar and easy. The suffering we experience in our lives seems natural to us. Everyone is doing it, thereby making it acceptable. Yes, there is agony, but we tell ourselves that there is ecstasy, too!

Now, Cypher begins to play the snake-in-the-grass with Neo. He says, "I'm going to let you in on a little secret here. Now don't tell him I told you this, but this ain't the first time Morpheus thought he found the One."

"Don't tell him I told you this," is a term often used by gossiping manipulators. Cypher has a hidden agenda, one that we will soon learn about.

Cypher tells Neo that there have been another five who Morpheus thought were "the One" before him. But Morpheus was wrong, and all of them are dead, killed by an Agent of the Matrix. By relaying this information, Cypher has successfully planted the seeds of doubt in Neo's head.

Cypher as Judas

Within the previous dialog, we can see that the Wachowskis have established Cypher as playing out the role of Judas Iscariot. He betrays Neo, Morpheus, and – in the grand scheme of things – the Truth (or, at least, the pursuit of truth). We next see Cypher dining with Agent Smith, who is attempting to entice Cypher to be the Matrix's mole on the Nebuchadnezzar.

In a very telling piece of dialog in *The Matrix*, Cypher says to the agent, "You know, I know that this steak doesn't exist. I know when I put it in my mouth, the Matrix is telling my brain that it is juicy and delicious. After nine years, do you know what I've realized? Ignorance is bliss."

Yes, for some the pursuit of Truth is too arduous a path; they would rather remain in the illusion. Once again, this brings home the point to be wary of those who will do anything to keep their belief system intact.

In Zen circles, the idea of "blissful ignorance" is looked at in a positive light, as an aspirational goal. Zen masters call it attaining "beginner's mind" (shoshin). Putting away one's preconceptions and approaching life with an *open* and free mind is a doorway to enlightenment. The thought goes that much of the world's learning is based on falsehoods, competition, and petty hatreds.

Zen masters would maintain that it seems healthier and more reasonable to take life one step at a time, which, after all, is what we do, anyway, even if we don't realize it!

This idea of blissful ignorance differs from what is advocated by Cypher. He prefers to live in denial of truth; he would rather live the lie. He admits to knowing that the steak doesn't exist, yet he luxuriates in that very same illusion.

It is of note that even though he knows the difference between truth and illusion while he is sitting there, he is consciously rejecting truth as he demands some ultimatums for his help. One of the prerequisites for helping the agents is that he wants complete forgetfulness for his past deeds while being given a life of luxury. Cypher doesn't want to take responsibility for his actions, opting for forgetfulness and remaining in a taxing, toxic form of "blissful ignorance."

Food Fight

In the next scene, the Wachowskis show the Nebuchadnezzar's crew having a meal. In the shooting script for *The Matrix*, the Wachowskis describe the food as "a substance with a consistency somewhere between yogurt and cellulite." Unappetizing, especially in contrast to the sumptuous meal that Cypher was eating in the previous scene.

While this contrast seems purposeful, we need not over-interpret it to mean that higher-minded truth seekers need to deny themselves the "finer" things in life. Cream of Wheat is no more or less "spiritual" than steak. Many on spiritual paths find that their tastes do become simpler, but what seems more important is that the emotional investment in the things of the world starts to dissolve. The "need" to have the "best" food, car, or clothes softens, becoming mere "preferences."

Now, it's Mouse's – a more minor player on the Nebuchadnezzar – turn to make a profound epistemic point. In discussing the bland meals they are fed on board, Mouse points out: "...you have to wonder, how do the machines know what Cream of Wheat really tasted like? Maybe they got it wrong, maybe what I think Cream of Wheat tasted like actually tasted like oatmeal, or tuna fish. It makes you wonder about a lot of things. Take chicken for example. Maybe they couldn't figure out what to make chicken taste like which is why chicken tastes like everything."

More broadly, everything is subjective. Taste is not inherent, it is learned through inculcation and by contrasting A with B, and then B with C, and so on. Various combinations of sweet, sour, bitter, and salty

– along with different textures – are ultimately all learned labels, not inherent states of being. Pretzels, we learn, are "salty," but if we were taught they are "sour," we would say "pretzels are sour."

The food for the Nebuchadnezzar's crew may well have been scientifically engineered for maximum nutritional value. But, because it was designed by a machine, the taste was bland – a weak attempt at creating something that would appeal to the crew.

Mouse plays philosopher again at the end of this scene. Whether it is our desire for tasty food or our longing for sexual satisfaction, Mouse asserts: "To deny our impulses is to deny the very thing that makes us human."

Many who have meditated or practiced other contemplative approaches have, in effect, trained their minds to "watch" their thoughts. The dull roar that we call "our thoughts" flood by at such a rapid clip that we often are not fully aware of them. Many spiritualities teach us that these thoughts imprison us, as they are at root different forms of fear, often "telling us" that we "lack" something, something we deserve or need.

These fear and lack thoughts come from our lower selves, what some call the "ego." Ego thoughts are often depressing, irritating, and sometimes infuriating. But Mouse makes an excellent point about our humanity: Denying ego thoughts is not helpful. Psychologically, that is repression or sublimation. We would have to look at those thoughts squarely, accept them as they are, and then go beyond them to find the truth to free our minds from delusions.

On the other hand, what "makes us human" is a notion the movie *The Matrix* very much challenges. Mr. Anderson *thought* he was a "human" when he was working as a programmer, after all!

The "needs" of the body are things that keep us bound up in the illusion, thinking that they are real and that we are really human beings. In a sense, we could view *The Matrix* as less a tale of enlightenment and more a story about the *first step toward enlightenment*.

We're Off to See the Oracle

Morpheus enters and announces that he will be taking Neo to see the Oracle. There is a famous story about the Oracle of Delphi, where she claimed that Socrates, much to his chagrin, was the "wisest" man around. After some thought, Socrates concluded that she was correct, for he *was* very wise in recognizing his own ignorance. His profound humility made him all the wiser. Ignorance, in this sense, *is* bliss!

While in transit to see the Oracle, Neo shares with Trinity that he has certain sentimental memories of his former life, deeply ensconced in the Matrix as he had been. "I have these memories, from my entire life but...none of them really happened," he tells her. "What does that mean?"

Trinity responds, "That the Matrix cannot tell you who you are."

The Wachowskis are setting us up again, by having Neo say next, "But an Oracle can."

Trinity adds, "That's different."

There's irony in this piece of dialog. For – while we can learn from others, including "authorities" like the Oracle – the source of all knowing ultimately *has to be* ourselves. We cannot delegate what we know and believe to another, for even if we defer to another who seems to possess greater insight than ourselves, it is still up to the individual to accept or reject the transfer of knowledge.

Put another way, even acquiescence is not really acquiescence! No matter how much one defers to another, an individual choice is being made in one's own mind. It's unavoidable.

All that to say that the Oracle, along with the Matrix, cannot tell you who you are, it is up to the individual to find the truth of who he or she really is.

The Tao of "Right" and "Wrong"
As this trip to see the Oracle proceeds, Neo asks a question about her that sounds like a statement. Neo says of the Oracle, "And she's never wrong." Wisely, Morpheus responds, "Don't think of it in terms of right and wrong. She is a guide, Neo. She can help you find the path."

This is reminiscent of the deeper meaning of a verse in the *Tao Te Ching*:

> *"When the world knows beauty as beauty, ugliness arises*
> *When it knows good as good, evil arises."*[4]

Labeling something "right" means – even creates the idea – that there is a "wrong." "Beauty" is then in automatic contrast with "ugliness." And that which is "good" means something must be "evil." It is inescapable within the dualistic world that we live in, where we find meaning through contrast. Another way to see how we base all judgment through contrasts, consider the opposite case. If all were right and there were no wrong, then there would be no contrast. All would simply just "be."

The meaning of the Tao translates to the "way," or the "path." And it is this that Morpheus is pointing Neo toward. To put it more forcefully, rather that judging that which unfolds before us, labeling things "right" or "wrong," would it not be wiser to find the next step on the path that feels virtuous and most helpful? Stopping to survey the damages feels morose and counter-productive. Best to keep moving on the path.

Sometimes, we need guidance when the next step along the path is not so obvious. This is the role that the Oracle, seers, and sages, and even everyday friends can play.

Doubting Thomas

As they approach the Oracle's apartment, Neo shares with Morpheus his doubts that meeting the Oracle will be any help, as a matter of fact, he is doubting pretty much everything. Neo is having a nihilistic moment. "The world I grew up in isn't real," he tells Morpheus. "My entire life was a lie. I don't believe in anything anymore."

This is of course understandable. We presume that Neo's life prior to meeting Trinity and Morpheus was an ordinary one for most growing up in Western culture. Be a good boy, study hard, get a good job, go to church, fear God...these are the elements that begin to explain pandemic neuroses, depression, and anger. To find as he has that his very existence was a lie makes it easy for him to over-react, to cocoon into a deeply skeptical, numbed-up nihilism.

Let's keep in mind, though, that Neo is at this stage still very much a newborn, one who is just getting used to this new and extraordinary existence. Who'd be in the mood to discover that he or she is supposed to save the world when his or her world has been thoroughly turned upside down?

Neo becomes somewhat shrill about this setup: "...I'm supposed to save the world? It sounds insane. Unbelievable. And I don't care who says it, it's still going to sound insane and unbelievable."

But Morpheus provides an answer, one that sidesteps Neo's myriad doubts. "Faith is not a matter of reasonability," he proclaims. "I do not believe things with my mind. I believe them with my heart. In my gut."

These words again should not be taken literally. We assume that mind resides in the brain, that thought is processed there. But do we know that for a fact? Researchers study what goes on in the brain and their conclusions are that, yes, the brain is where thought happens. But, on the other hand, as Ramana Maharshi taught, even if we try to trace our thoughts back to their source, in truth we really cannot know where thought comes from. Many who meditate notice that emotion seems to either arise in the heart and even the gut, but ultimately the mind remains a mystery.

Still, we can understand the perspective that Morpheus is pointing to. Our mind – whatever and wherever it is – seems divided into what might be called an analytical side (some call it the "left brain") which assembles facts, theories, and observations. Then we have an emotional side (sometimes called the "right brain"), where creativity and imagination rule. Morpheus clearly prefers this latter, emotional, right-brained approach.

Mistaken Messiahs

Neo is still not satisfied. Part of his doubts about Morpheus and the Oracle spring from what Cypher told him earlier – that he is the sixth "One" that Morpheus has championed. "What about the other five guys?" Neo asks Morpheus. "The five before me? What about them?"

Like the rare, contrite politician, Morpheus hesitatingly admits: "I believed what the Oracle told me...no, I misunderstood what she told me. I believed that it was all about me."

Morpheus delves deeper into the hubris he once had: "I believed that all I had to do was point my finger and anoint whoever I chose. I was wrong, Neo. Terribly wrong. Not a day or night passes that I do not think of them. After the fifth, I lost my way. I doubted everything the Oracle had said. I doubted myself."

Is this a sincere confession? Did these five prior, false "Ones" trigger Morpheus into his own form of self-doubting nihilism? Or is Morpheus manipulating Neo? Almost like what's called "love at first sight," Morpheus exclaims that "my world changed" on seeing Neo, that it was an "epiphany."

As stated earlier, Neo has long had "trust issues," which Morpheus addresses directly by saying to him: "...all I am asking from you is for you to hold on to whatever respect you may have for me and trust me."

It does seem that Morpheus recognizes that his withholding the fact that Neo is the sixth "One" broke trust; it was a sin of omission. Still, Neo – by all indications – seems to buy Morpheus's confession.

Home is Where the Heart Is

Once inside the Oracle's apartment, Neo is shown around by a Priestess and is introduced to children whom she calls the Potentials. One is levitating alphabet blocks, while another – a boy with a shaved head, looking like a Zen monk – is bending spoons.

As Neo crosses the room to approach the spoon-bending boy, in the frame we can see Neo's upside-down reflection in the spoon. A nice foreshadowing, as Neo's world has been generally turned upside down.

The boy hands Neo the now-straight spoon, saying, "Do not try to bend the spoon. That is impossible. Instead, only try to realize the truth."

Again with this "truth" stuff. When they first met, Morpheus suggested to Neo that "[i]t is the world that has been pulled over your eyes to blind you from the truth." To which Neo asked, "What truth?" Neo asks the boy the same question, "What truth?"

In one of the most profound moments in film history, the boy calmly, matter-of-factly answers, "There is no spoon."

This may sound daft, delusional. And yet for those who have studied non-dual metaphysics, it makes perfect sense.

For example, one of the most powerful exponents of the non-dual concept, Indian sage Sri Nisargadatta Maharaj, put it this way: "As there must be something unchanging to register discontinuity, I am not this body-mind, which is neither continuous nor permanent." In other words, if we perceive a world that appears to be constantly changing and in motion, there must be something that is constant, immutable, and unchanging. There has to be a standard against which all change and motion is measured, registered. Two bodies in motion perceiving each other cannot gauge the other's movement unless there is some universal yardstick.

The spoon and literally everything in the material world had a beginning. It is only the eternal that is real, according to non-dualism. There is no spoon, not really, because the only thing that is truly real is the beginning-less, endless eternal. As Nisargadatta put it, "Only reality is, there is nothing else." And what you may ask is reality? That which has no beginning or end, the eternal present.

Everything else is Strawberry Fields *redux*, where "nothing is real."

Neo, ever the questioning student, repeats, "There is no spoon." With a hint of a question mark in Reeves's delivery, we get the sense that Neo seems earnest enough, although he has some skepticism. He is, after all, being asked to deny what his eyes see as plain as day. Still, Neo is open minded; he doesn't hesitate to try (successfully) to bend the spoon himself – only to be interrupted by the Priestess, who ushers him in to see the Oracle.

The Oracle asks Neo, "So? What do you think? You think you're the One?

Predictably, Neo responds, "Honestly? I don't know."

She points to a wooden plaque, written in Latin, which reads, "Know Thyself." In history, this was perhaps the best known of all the Delphic Maxims, sayings that the Oracle of Delphi transmitted from the Greek God Apollo.

The Oracle expounds: "I'm gonna let you in on a little secret. Being the One is just like being in love. Nobody can tell you you're in love. You just know it. Through and through. Balls to bones."

After some cryptic to and fro, Neo offers the concession that he is not, in fact, the One. The Oracle's response is clever. She says, "Sorry, kid. You got the gift but looks like you're waiting for something...Your next life, maybe. Who knows?"

Neo's – Thomas's! – doubting mind hears that he's *not* the One. However, The Oracle has not actually said that. She has left things vague. The Oracle goes on to predict that Morpheus will ultimately sacrifice his own life to save Neo's. But that Neo will be faced with a choice, one in which he can sacrifice his life to save Morpheus.

By planting seeds and connecting *some* dots for Neo, The Oracle is leading Neo toward Truth without actually putting it all out there on a silver platter for him. She knows that he *is* in fact the One, but that because he doesn't believe it, he *isn't* the One. He's not ready, and nothing she tells him will convince him otherwise.

After they reunite, Morpheus wisely tells Neo, "You don't have to tell anyone what she told you. What was said was said for you and you alone." We can't know if Morpheus knows what was said, but he does know how this often-cryptic game is played. Neo keeps what was said secret, at least for now.

Deja Vu, Too

Morpheus, Neo, and the team make their way back to the Nebuchadnezzar. On the way, Neo spots a black cat crossing the threshold, and then, moments later, an identical cat follows in the first's footsteps. Neo says out-loud, *"deja vu."*

To Neo's surprise, Trinity takes this comment very seriously, asking, "Was it the same cat?" She goes on to explain that when a *deja vu* happens it represents a "glitch" in the Matrix. The machines that run the Matrix have often changed something.

These alterations in the Matrix's space/time continuum trigger fear in Trinity, for she has experienced *deja vu* before, and the results were never good.

A Stitch in Time

Here the Wachowskis nod to both physicists and meta-physicists who, in different ways, posit that time is actually an illusion. From Buddhists to Christian mystics like Meister Eckhart, some suggest that time is a matter that needs much investigation. Eckhart for instance wrote, "There exists only the present instant ... There is no yesterday nor any tomorrow, but only Now...."

Albert Einstein also had some thoughts about the illusory nature of time. "The only reason for time is so that everything doesn't happen at once," he once said. Time may be something akin to the eternal revealing itself in bite-sized chunks. Some physicists postulate that time and space are actually a hologram, all happening at once but that we "stretch" it out and perceive it linearly.

Coming at this question from another direction, Einstein has also said, "When forced to summarize the general theory of relativity in one sentence: Time and space and gravitation have no separate existence from matter."

Einstein could be pointing us to some *thing* that is tantamount to a pantheistic God, some universal oneness that contains all things eternally, without change. We could think of it as ubiquitous, unwavering love.

From this timeless, immutable love perspective, there are no problems – nothing is amiss. In time, however, there are always things to do, dysfunctions to fix. When the machines make a change to the Matrix, it appears like a botched splice in the film that we are watching. In this case, Neo sees the same cat cross the threshold two times.

Throughout much of *The Matrix*, we see Neo wanting desperately to be in "control" of his life. But at some cosmic level, it could be that what we call our "lives" are entirely – for lack of a better term – pre-ordained. His struggle for control could well be, in a sense, futile.

After The Oracle again leads Neo to believe that he's not the One, she left him with these parting thoughts, "You'll remember that you don't believe any of this fate crap. You're in control of your own life, remember?"

Recall that when he first met Morpheus, Neo stated he didn't believe in "fate" because he didn't like the *idea* that he wasn't in control of his own life.

Run Away to Fight Another Day
Trinity was correct, something had changed in the Matrix, and they were in trouble. As the team is confronted with a helicopter, cops, and machine-gun fire by the agents, now is not the time for metaphysical pondering about glitches, but evasive action!

And escape they do, all except for Morpheus, who is captured by the agents. The rest of the team seek to return to the Nebuchadnezzar via the telephone transporter setup that's used throughout *The Matrix*. Cypher – the Judas of the story – has other plans. He shoots Tank and Dozer, and then reveals to Trinity – who is still in the Matrix – that he is up to no good.

Benedict Cypher
Cypher is especially resentful of Morpheus. He feels that this red-pill Real World is not all that Morpheus represented it to be. And, like Neo earlier in the film, Cypher has his own trust issues with authority figures, which we can see from the following dialog.

When Trinity asserts that Morpheus has set them all free, Cypher shoots back, "Free? You call this free? All I do is what he tells me to do. If I have to choose between that and the Matrix, I choose the Matrix."

Paraphrasing Einstein, the "reality" of the Matrix is sufficiently persistent for Cypher to prefer it over the hellish reality of the Real World. Cypher tells Trinity that Agent Smith has promised to re-insert him into the Matrix, where, "I'll go back to sleep and when I wake up, I'll be fat and rich and I won't remember a goddamned thing. It's the American dream."

What Goes Around...

Cypher telegraphs to Trinity over the phone that he's about to kill Switch by unplugging her body back on the Nebuchadnezzar. He does so, and then sets his sights on Neo. He taunts Trinity, asking her, "If Neo is the One, then in the next few seconds there has to be some kind of miracle to stop me. Right? How can he be the One if he's dead?"

Some have asked the same sorts of questions regarding the story of Jesus' death. If he was *really* the one Son of God, surely he could get off the cross if he so willed it. Of course, the story goes that he *had* to die to absolve the rest of us for our sins.

This set up by the Wachowskis is quite rich. Cypher cruelly asks Trinity if she really believed "Morpheus's bullshit" that Neo is the One. She, of course, answers "Yes," stating her belief forthrightly.

Being a Hollywood movie, we've come to expect that the "bad guy," in this case Cypher, will get what's coming to him. This comes in the convenient form that Tank did not actually die. Instead, Tank stands, gun in hand. On seeing this, Cypher exclaims, "I don't believe it!"

And Tank responds, with righteousness in his voice, "Believe it or not, you piece of shit, you're still going to burn." Tank could easily have said, "...burn in Hell," two additional words that seem inferred.

The miracle that Cypher mocked moments ago happens. We see the maxim, "What goes around, comes around," play out quite quickly in this case. Underneath this sequence of events, it's notable that the Wachowskis illustrate the power of belief so plainly and powerfully. Trinity and Tank's single-pointed and virtuous belief overpowers Cypher's jaded *dis*belief in dramatic, deadly fashion.

Nothing New Under the Sun

Neo and Trinity return via phone lines to reunite with Tank. Still, there's the matter of Morpheus, who we next see being interrogated by Agent Smith. Smith reveals some of the machine's backstory to Morpheus. For example, the first Matrix was a "perfect human world," free of suffering, an eternally happy place. And, yet, this Matrix 1.0 was a disaster.

Agent Smith relays *why* it was a disaster. "[A]s a species," Smith tells Morpheus, "human beings define their reality through suffering and misery." This may be a bit harsh, but the impulse to commit self-sabotage seems undeniable. Freud referred to this tendency as the repetition compulsion. Too often, we are all our own worst enemies.

Recognizing this notion that humans define their reality through suffering and misery is a bracing philosophical stance for most. Many may cite romantic love, puppy dogs, and random acts of kindness as counters. But, if we are to connect Einstein's idea that time, space, and matter are all the same, then a deep sense of suffering seems entirely predictable.

Why? Because we perceive the universe to be made up of countless separated things, ever-changing through the passage of time. We could be – at a deep, unconscious level – completely wrong about everything! We think that a cosmic Big Bang actually happened, exploding the oneness of eternity when – if Einstein is fundamentally correct – this Big Bang didn't actually happen. It's more accurate to say it *appears* to have happened.

What the Buddhists identify as our self-imposed tendency to suffer (dukkha) comes about because it is postulated that the drama we call "the world" and "our life" is to be taken all too seriously. Who wins the Super Bowl, the presidency, or "big" conflicts are considered by most as "important." Whether we get the job, the girl, or the financing for that coveted new car can take on epic proportions in our minds. We invest in these outcomes, despite the fact that the results are, in the grand scheme of things, inconsequential.

Buddhists maintain that no matter what happens in time and space, the Oneness remains intact, in truth.

We are all watching (and enjoying, strangely enough) a movie entitled "life," that is filled with turmoil. Despite the fact that it's not in our interest to buy into this painful film, we watch this same crazy movie, over and over again, with each stage filled with seemingly different characters and situations. We just keep forgetting that "there is nothing new under the sun," (Ecclesiastes 1:9, KJV)

"I'm Going In"

Many Eastern spiritual philosophies refer to the belief in the material world (time, space, and matter) as "the separation." Specifically, it is a separation of man, flesh, and the physical world from the eternal spirit of God. From a non-dual perspective, the separation did not actually happen, it's an illusion, or "Maya," which is the Sanskrit term that posits the material world is a fantasy.

Neo, Trinity, and Tank – being a step removed from the illusory world of The Matrix – still believe that there are things that need to be done to make things right. With Morpheus being tortured, Tank concludes that Morpheus's body back on the Nebuchadnezzar should be unplugged, i.e., to effect a mercy killing. Trinity doesn't like the idea, and yet she seems to accede to Tank's solution. Neo seems paralyzed by the prospect. But, just before Tank pulls the plug on Morpheus, Neo shouts, "Stop!"

Neo relays to Trinity and Tank that the Oracle had prophesied this very development. She told him, Neo says, "That I would have to make a choice...." Neo trails off, not sharing with Trinity and Tank the Oracle's full prophesy from earlier in the film: "In one hand, you will have Morpheus's life. In the other hand, you will have your own. One of you is going to die. Which one, will be up to you."

Neo uses tact here, since he is preparing to sacrifice himself to save Morpheus's life as well as Zion itself. (Zion being the last stronghold of humanity in this Real World. This scene also establishes that Agent Smith is torturing Morpheus to get the codes to Zion's mainframe computer.)

Neo boldly proclaims: "I'm going in." Trinity strongly objects to this idea, but Neo explains that Morpheus has been laboring under the false assumption that Neo is the One. Neo tells her that the Oracle revealed this to him. "I'm not the One, Trinity," he tells her. "The Oracle hit me with that, too."

Reeves played this scene extremely well. He seems to have an epiphany, a moment in which he appears to receive a message. His head jerks in such a way that he hears, understands, and acts upon the clear guidance he's just received.

Tank catalogs all the obstacles Neo will face in attempting to go in and save Morpheus. Neo's firm response really cannot be countered: "I know that's what it looks like, but it's not. I can't logically explain to you why it's not. Morpheus believed something and he was ready to give his life for what he believed. I understand that now. That's why I have to go."

TANK: Why?

NEO: Because I believe in something.

TRINITY: What?

NEO: I believe I can bring him back.

A Choiceless Choice
Again, the Wachowskis use very simple statements and questions to underscore the power of determination and clarity. Neo is completely unconflicted in this scene. He has *no doubt* that he's doing the right thing. We could say that, in a sense, he has no choice. This must be done, in Neo's mind, despite the protestations of Tank and Trinity.

Inspired by Neo, Trinity decides that she too must go with him, despite *his* disapproval. Next, when Neo and Trinity prepare in the Construct to rescue Morpheus, they speak with Tank, and he asks them: "Okay. What do you need? Besides a miracle...."

This is the second mention of a miracle in *The Matrix*. Like the last mention of a miracle by a doubting Cypher, the thought of a miracle comes from the momentarily doubting player, Tank. Neo and Trinity have no doubts about this mission. Trinity indicates that what they are doing is unprecedented, Neo states with a quiet confidence, "That's why it's going to work."

A Little Gunplay

Neo and Trinity walk with great surety into the building where Morpheus is being held. When confronted by security guards, they pull out their arsenal of guns and acrobatic moves to drive past this obstacle.

Next, they rig the elevators in their quest to save Morpheus. During this sequence requiring great facility, Neo calmly states, "There is no spoon." This indicates that he is coming into his own. He is bringing the knowledge of the unreality of the Matrix *into* the Matrix, allowing him to eventually overcome the illusion.

To elaborate, Neo in his own way is walking through this "valley of the shadow of death," which looks like an impossible situation fearing no evil because, deep down, Neo knows that there is no spoon.

What does this mean? This film gives the impression that all of time and space is an illusion. He is, in a sense, playing his part to the best of his abilities *within* the illusion, while another part of his mind has *transcended* this dreamscape.

In short, he's *above the fray* while he seems to be deeply *in the fray*. And, because he is viewing the chaos from above, he recognizes that it is all just a trifling game. Oddly enough, this enables Neo to be far more effective on the battleground, as he is now open to inspiration and not weighed down by worry, fear, and doubt.

The battle continues on the rooftop. This is the scene where Neo has developed a startling ability: bullet dodging. When Trinity asks, "Neo, how did you do that?"

Neo doesn't really recognize his new, miraculous ability. "Do what?" he asks. Neo apparently didn't even know that he could move with that kind of speed, but as he really *is* becoming the One, he is increasingly practicing what Jed McKenna, author of *Spiritual Enlightenment: The Damnedest Thing* calls "releasing the tiller." He is letting go of the control that he has so tightly held onto for his entire life. As he does so, it could be viewed metaphysically that he is increasingly letting – let's call it – a Higher Power take control of his life.

Indeed, Neo maintains his humility, noting that he "wasn't fast enough" for he was, in fact, grazed by bullets. Next, Neo and Trinity commandeer a helicopter, and make a frontal, air-borne assault on the room where Morpheus is being held.

While it's a harrowing, over-the-top effort, they do rescue Morpheus – barely! Neo's physical accomplishment in saving them when the helicopter crashes is a profound one. For Trinity and Tank, this proves what Morpheus has known all along: Neo is the One.

Recall that Neo went into this effort to save Morpheus as an either/or proposition: one of them was going to die, and Neo made the decision that Morpheus's life was more important to the cause than his own. Unexpectedly, with his newfound abilities to traverse the Matrix effectively, he changes prophecy and they *both* live.

Face Your Fear

Before Neo can go back to the Nebuchadnezzar with the others, an old man on the platform transforms into Agent Smith who then faces Neo for a show-down. Neo's first instinct is to run, to head for the exits. Instead, he decides to confront Agent Smith and face his fear. The script put it this way:

> "Neo looks at the dead escalator that rises up behind him. Slowly he turns back and in his eyes we see something different, something fixed and hard like a gunfighter's resolve. There is no past or future in these eyes. There is only what is."

Back on the Nebuchadnezzar's main deck, Morpheus, Trinity, and Tank watch this drama unfolding on their screen. Trinity exclaims, "What is he doing?" Morpheus, with certainty, responds: "He's beginning to believe."

This arc for Neo has come to its apex. When we first meet him, he is a confused, exhausted seeker, someone for whom the splinter in his mind drives him to find answers. He becomes more focused with the help of his guru, Morpheus, and chooses the red pill of truth. Neo is then tested by the Oracle, who finds his resolve insufficient, with his doubts clouding his determination.

This leads to a crisis point – a moment where all will be lost: Morpheus, Zion, and the last vestiges of humanity. In that moment, in that darkest nadir, he is struck with "divine" inspiration. While saving Morpheus would appear to be a "sacrifice," it becomes an act of self-preservation. By saving Morpheus, he saves Zion, and, in the process, he saves himself. This does seem to be the way of it for the seeker of truth as well.

During this process, the training with Morpheus combined with Neo's gifts come into full flower. Now that he determined to save Morpheus, Neo himself received his own salvation. As ACIM puts it: "To give and to receive are one in truth."5 This idea goes against the teaching of the world, which believes in separate interests. Those separate interests are referred to in Kabbalah as "receiving for the self alone." But, given the non-dualistic pointers we see in *The Matrix*, a universal oneness starts to make the ideas of "giving" and "receiving" meaningless. They are in fact, one and the same, as illustrated by Neo's selfless act. This was clearly a win-win situation!

Know Thyself...More and More

Now, it seems, Neo has an inkling of who he really is. He sees through the nature of the Matrix knowing it to be an illusion, thus freeing up his mind within it. His fear of Agent Smith is gone. He acts with a quiet confidence, beginning to truly believe that he is the One.

A titanic battle ensues between Agent Smith and Neo. At one point, Agent Smith haughtily proclaims that the sound of the approaching train is the "sound of inevitability." Thinking he has finally won, Smith says, "Good-bye, Mr. Anderson."

"My name is Neo," again underscoring that Neo knows who he really is, not some identity made up in the illusory world of this Matrix. Neo turns the tables in spectacular fashion, sending Agent Smith to be run over by the train. Limping, Neo goes for the escalator, as another incarnation of Agent Smith now exits the subway car.

By doing so, the Wachowskis point to the idea that this waking-up business is not a neat and tidy process. It is more journey than destination, for challenges and tests are a lifelong pursuit. Neo may now be well along the way toward enlightenment, but the ego (in its many forms in this Matrix) is nothing if not persistent!

Neo makes his way to the abandoned Heart O' the City hotel. Tank has dialed the phone, Neo hears it ringing as he frantically searches for the room with the correct phone. He opens a door in hopes it's where the phone is, but inside is Agent Smith, holding a gun. In a flash, Neo is shot, falling to the ground. By all indications, he's dead.

Love Conquers All

Believing that this time, Neo is *really* dead, Agent Smith reprises what he said to Neo in the subway station. "Good-bye, Mr. Anderson," he smirks.

It'd be supremely anti-climactic if Neo were to die here, like this! So here is where we learn that "love conquers all." On the main deck,

Trinity whispers to the wired-up husk of Neo's body that sits in the chair: "You can't be dead, Neo, you can't be because I love you. You hear me? I love you!"

As the script says:

> Her eyes close and she kisses him, believing in all her heart that he will feel her lips and know that they speak the truth.
>
> He does. And they do.
>
> His eyes snap open.

First crucified, Neo is now resurrected! This third miracle is his most extraordinary in the film, which garner him some newfound powers. He has completely embraced his true nature, he knows who he is and cannot be constrained by the Matrix any longer.

It is a metaphysically poignant moment. His resurrection claims that even though the body dies in the Matrix (in the illusion), that he (mankind) is so much more. We have a glimpse of the eternal nature of spirit that cannot be quelled by the death of the body.

Neo rises and we see the Agents at the other end of the hall. Shocked at the sight of an alive Mr. Anderson, they draw their weapons and blast away at this resurrected ghost.

Neo raises his hands, and commandingly says, "No!" His will is now *so* strong that the bullets stop in their tracks, mid-air. They fall harmlessly to the floor.

To illustrate that something has dramatically changed about Neo, he no longer sees the Matrix as the rest of us do. His perception has shifted to see through the illusion. Neo now views the Matrix for what it is: auras of computer code. The veil of Maya has been lifted.

Completely enraged, Agent Smith rushes toward Neo, unleashing a ferocious martial attack. Having reached that place of being "in the world, but not of it," Neo nonchalantly blunts each blow. And, then, with one swift, certain strike to the chest, Neo sends Agent Smith flying down the hallway.

Brilliantly from a non-dual perspective, the Wachowskis don't have Neo go and beat Agent Smith to a pulp. Since all is one, Neo instead *dives into* Agent Smith, becomes one with him. Smith becomes completely discombobulated, while the confines of his body seem to melt and distort. And then Neo re-emerges from Agent Smith, and body of the agent dissolves into beams of light.

Hollywood Ending

Of course, we are treated to a Hollywood ending now. Neo gets back to the phone in a nick of time, just as the sentinels have stormed the Nebuchadnezzar. Morpheus triggers the EMP, zapping the sentinels with a white-light energy pulse.

Neo regains consciousness back on the main deck, and is promptly treated to a welcoming kiss from Trinity. All is well with the world, at least for now.

As stated earlier, the path of enlightenment is more journey than destination. As the Zen proverb goes, "Before enlightenment: Chop wood, carry water. After enlightenment: Chop wood, carry water."

And so the Wachowskis end *The Matrix* as they began it: A simple computer screen, with blinking cursor. (The final cut of the film differs from the following script version, with Neo's lines substantially shortened. Still, the script version has more revealing dialog, so it is discussed here.) There is streaming computer code, with Neo delivering some voice-over parting thoughts. Whether this last piece of dialog is:

- A monolog (a speech given to an audience. As in: "Friends, Romans, countrymen, lend me your ears"),

or a

- A soliloquy (a speech that one gives to oneself. As in: "To be, or not to be – that is the question")

is a very interesting question. At first, Neo seems to be addressing the machines, the artificial intelligence responsible for making the Matrix:

NEO (V.O. [voice-over]): You won't have to search for me anymore. I'm done running. Done hiding. Whether I'm done fighting, I suppose, is up to you.

Then, it seems that the focus of Neo's words and whom he is addressing changes.

NEO (V.O.): I believe deep down, we both want this world to change. I believe that the Matrix can remain our cage or it can become our chrysalis, that's what you helped me to understand. That to be free, you cannot change your cage. You have to change yourself.

These words seem more directed at viewers of *The Matrix*. Non-dualism can be tricky stuff, since oneness envisions neither subject nor object. All is one, after all!

The counsel about changing yourself rather than your cage is a theme one sees in many non-dualistic paths. ACIM, for example, says: "Seek not to change the world, but choose to change your mind about the world."[6]

Neo continues:

> NEO (V.O.): When I used to look out at this world, all I could see was its edges, its boundaries, its rules and controls, its leaders and laws. But now, I see another world. A different world where all things are possible. A world of hope. Of peace. I can't tell you how to get there, but I know if you can free your mind, you'll find the way.

As Neo tells us, "deep down" we all want this world to change. The gauntlet that *The Matrix* lays down is that this often underlying – sometimes subconscious – desire cannot be done without first recognizing that the "fault" is not with "the stars," but "in ourselves." Specifically, the fault is in our *mind*; we imprison ourselves in a Construct of our *own* making!

As Einstein so eloquently put it, "The significant problems we face cannot be solved at the same level of thinking we were at when we created them."

The final image of Neo blasting off like Superman may seem hackneyed for some, but its powerful imagery suggests that Neo has himself, first, recognized his *cage* as *chrysalis*. He is no longer a victim of his circumstances, for he has come to recognize – in this trial by fire – that *there is no spoon*. Neo now knows that he is responsible for his "circumstances" since his situation is entirely his interpretation of the edges and boundaries that he sees in the world. And, most importantly, he recognizes that these boundaries are false!

There's no need to view *The Matrix* or any other film that deals with spiritual or metaphysical matters with literalistic, academic rigor. In fact, we can end up inappropriately poking holes in a film's intellectual content when the film's purpose is to entertain and stimulate us emotionally, first and foremost. The Wachowskis are filmmakers, not academics, but that they weave together profound philosophical insights makes *The Matrix* all the more satisfying than most popcorn fare.

The Matrix was a commercial, money-making movie, a smash hit, in fact. However, the alluring, enduring power of the story springs from a non-dualistic, metaphysical, and spiritual foundation. While most of those who've viewed *The Matrix* have probably not read Eckhart Tolle, much less Ramana Maharshi, workaday viewers were likely moved at some level by the deeper themes in this filmic masterpiece.

Progress – real progress – begins when we recognize that *there is no spoon.*

Endnotes for *The Matrix*

1. Film Scouts, "The Matrix: Casting," www.filmscouts.com/scripts/matinee.cfm?Film=matrix&File=casting

2. Jed McKenna, *Spiritual Warfare*, (Lexington, KY: Wisefool Press, 2012), p. 127

3. Kenneth Wapnick, Ph.D., "The Body - An Engine of Destruction," Foundation for A Course in Miracles, https://www.facebook.com/PublisherOfACIM/posts/358416190850717

4. Laozi, *Tao Te Ching*, (Woodstock, VT: SkyLight Paths Publishing, 2006), p.5

5. *A Course in Miracles*, (Glen Ellen, CA: Foundation for Inner Peace, 1992) W-108

6. *A Course in Miracles*, (Glen Ellen, CA: Foundation for Inner Peace, 1992) T-27.1:7

Dark City: Forget the Sun. Forget Time. Forget Your Memories.

Often overlooked, *Dark City* is among the greatest metaphysical movies in the modern era. Released in 1998 – a year before *The Matrix* – several reviewers have suggested that *Dark City* is a "Gnostic" film, which certainly makes a lot of sense.[1][2] *(See Appendix C for more on Gnosticism.)*

A case could also be made that *Dark City* illustrates the idea of "leela" from the Hindu tradition. Vedic (a school of Hinduism) philosophers held that the material world is an illusion, but that the illusion is manipulated by God for sport, to amuse Him or to teach us life lessons.

The contemporary *A Course in Miracles (ACIM)* also posits that the material world is illusory, since it suggests that that which is not eternal is not real. Only love – universal, abstract love – is eternal, making the material world, in a sense, illusory because of its changing nature.

Dark City's narrative is more along the lines of a quest, mixed in with a detective story. The film's protagonist is John Murdoch (played by Rufus Sewell), although Murdoch doesn't even know his name at the film's outset.

Murdoch is the one man who is beginning to wake up among a population of sleepwalkers. When we meet him, he literally awakens...in a bathtub. Like the first self-aware human might have been, Murdoch wakes up shocked and confused. He doesn't know who or where he is. Not surprisingly, he is naked, in many ways symbolic of what the first living, conscious person might be like, newly born yet with well-developed faculties. He knows how to do the things of life, like dressing himself, but he doesn't have an identity of any kind. The bathtub's water, too, is symbolic of the womb of life.

As he gathers himself, Murdoch finds some clothes and a suitcase with the initials "K.M." Murdoch's worldly identity begins to reveal itself, albeit quite slowly. He finds a postcard for a vacation spot called "Shell Beach." This triggers a vivid burst of a memory that is interrupted by a ringing phone.

It's a person who says he's a doctor, speaking quickly and urgently. The doctor (whom we later learn is Dr. Schreber, played by Kiefer Sutherland) tells Murdoch that he's been the victim of an experiment, one that erased Murdoch's memory. Schreber implores Murdoch to leave – quickly, as some unnamed people are coming to get him.

Murdoch is, in a sense, *tabula rasa*, a man with no identity, no history, no personal story. As he begins to gather his bearings, he discovers a dead woman's body on the floor of his hotel room. Even more perplexing, her half-naked body is painted with spirals, implying that his search for his identity in *Dark City* will be complicated.

As Murdoch leaves the hotel room, three shadowy figures come walking down the hall. These are the people Schreber warned Murdoch about, and he avoids this encounter.

Truth Sets Us Free, but What is Truth?

With this opening sequence, *Dark City*'s director and co-screenwriter Alex Proyas (*The Crow, I, Robot*) seems to be establishing that our worldly identities are in no way absolute truths, but rather learned and, in a sense, contrived. While we derive comfort from our names, personalities, and professional reputations, none of these are "true" in the absolute sense. What would it be like to be a newborn with no "story" about who we are? This person that we will come to know as "Murdoch" is just such a person, seeing the world through completely fresh eyes.

As Murdoch goes down to the hotel lobby, oddly, everyone there is asleep...in a phone booth, on couches, and at the clerk's desk. Murdoch checks with the just-awoken clerk at the front desk. The clerk then wakes and addresses him as "Murdoch," the first instance in which Murdoch will start putting together his previous identity. Apparently, John has lost his wallet, but the clerk reports that the Automat called saying that they have his billfold. He exits the hotel to retrieve the wallet.

Proyas uses this hotel clerk to illustrate – in a small way – the utter senselessness of what people do sometimes. Despite his telling Murdoch that his wallet is at the Automat – presumably carrying the cash needed to pay his hotel bill – the clerk proceeds to go to Murdoch's room to evict him. Contradictory behavior! Presumably, on his return with the wallet, Murdoch would have paid his bill.

This blind rule-following doesn't work out for the clerk, as he encounters the three shadowy figures who are looking for Murdoch. After interrogating him about Murdoch, they put the clerk to sleep with a wave of a hand.

The Search for Self Begins

Next, we meet Emma Murdoch (played by Jennifer Connolly), a nightclub singer, while on stage. After her set, she gets a business card backstage that a Dr. Schreber has left for her, leaving the message that he is her husband's doctor, and that he wants to speak with her at his office.

Emma goes to see Schreber, who explains that Murdoch may be "delusional, even violent." As Schreber literally puts a rat in a maze (furthering the theme established by the complexity of the spirals in the previous scene), he explains that Murdoch is unwell psychologically, a fact of which Emma is unaware.

"Wherever your husband is," Schreber concludes, "he is searching...for himself," which is itself a spiritually pregnant comment. Aren't we all, in a sense?! And search Murdoch does. We cut to him pacing on a darkened street, uttering possible names for himself.

Brilliantly, Proyas has Murdoch walking in front of storefront mannequins, as he rehearses what the "J" stands for in his name, which he learned from the hotel registry: J Murdoch. Jake, Justin, Jerry, Jason, John...he tries them all on for his "audience" of mannequins. He finds this all funny, as he lets out a little laugh. He recognizes how his mildly schizophrenic behavior appears when his vocal diatribe is interrupted by a street sweeper, who appears out of the darkness. Murdoch stops his search for his identity (for the moment) as he recognizes that his behavior appears a bit loopy. To the street sweeper (who never acknowledges him), Murdoch weakly says, "Hi," and then lets out a little "huh," as he turns on his heel and walks away.

This short sequence illustrates how meticulous Proyas is as a filmmaker. With overtones of the Indian Advaita Vedanta sage, Ramana Maharshi, as well as other spiritual philosophers, the search for truth begins with the question, "Who am I?" Proyas has set this question up nicely in this allegorical film. In a world populated with mannequins, all that seems to be left is the consciousness in our heads. Stripped of all preconceptions, the fundamental question we can ask is: Who am I?

We assume we are a person with the name that our parents gave us. That we are short, tall, skinny, fat, of a certain age, a certain gender. As we go through life, we collect experiences and use them to define who we think we are. For example, we might go to college, join the military, start a family, etc. But with profound amnesia, Murdoch plays out Ramana's "who am I?" with filmic panache, as well as with an understandable anxious feeling of alienation.

All Yin-and-Yang Here in Dark City

Now we meet Inspector Bumstead (played by William Hurt). As we learn, unlike Murdoch's identity crisis, Bumstead seems to know who he is. As we are introduced to the inspector, he is seated and playing an accordion. The black-and-white keyboard and baffles are the first indication of the dualistic character that he plays. To further establish this two-fold personality, we see in the background a fireplace mantle that has a metronome and a black-and-white picture of a woman, possibly his mother. Proyas seems to be implying that Bumstead has a very distinct yin-and-yang/black-and-white worldview.

An old-style, black-and-white, rotary phone rings, causing Bumstead to stop playing. Bumstead turns to us with a blank look on his face as he picks up the phone. He's being called in for a murder investigation.

Cut to Murdoch outside the Automat. He's still highly disoriented, a situation made worse by the cook behind the glass who only seems to be able to answer questions evasively. (Can't we all relate on some level to dealing with cryptic service people?) The cook puts Murdoch's lost wallet in one of the vending slots. Proyas begins to reveal to us that Murdoch is beginning to display extraordinary abilities in this bewildering dark city, where many things seem jumbled and out of place. Murdoch focuses his mind on the Automat door, and with his mind alone he is able to pop it open to retrieve his wallet.

Now we find Bumstead beginning his investigation of a hooker's murder. It is the same woman who Murdoch found in his hotel room. Bumstead is steely-eyed and competent, assessing the murder scene clinically and effectively. As he focuses on a goldfish swimming in the tub, he wonders aloud: "So, Hasselbeck, what kind of killer do you think stops to save a dying fish?"

Three Archetypes

The name "Bumstead" seems to be in stark contrast to the way Hurt plays the role. We're reminded of Dagwood Bumstead from the cartoon strip *Blondie* – kind of a goofy, hapless character who is hard to take seriously. Hurt, on the other hand, with his rendition of Inspector Bumstead, is at his most serious and dead-panned.

The contrast between Murdoch and Bumstead is key. Murdoch stumbles around, and yet he also displays extraordinary powers. Bumstead, on the other hand, seems highly in control of his faculties and environment, but he lacks any of the special abilities that Murdoch possesses. In a sense, Murdoch is spiritually awakening, while Bumstead is quite asleep, spiritually speaking.

Inspector Bumstead is replacing the last inspector on the case, Inspector Walenski (played by Colin Friels). Apparently there has been a string of serial call-girl murders that has gripped the city, and even though Inspector Walenski is no longer in charge, he seems to be especially troubled by what is happening. He bursts through the police lines, raving to Bumstead, "There's no way out!"

In another scene, light, cheery music ironically follows Bumstead as he pays a visit to Walenski's office. Bumstead is starting to reveal a victim type of consciousness lying underneath his competent exterior. At one point he says: "I'm being punished for my sins," when confronted with the unkempt craziness of Walenski's office, where the walls are covered by deranged scribbles and newspaper clippings. This victim mentality begins to explain the joyless, going-through-the-motions veneer that is Bumstead's personality.

Later, Bumstead is handed fingerprints from the murder scene. But these are no ordinary fingerprints, for the patterns are spirals, spirals like those found on the murder victims that Bumstead is investigating. "What is this," Bumstead says, "some kind of joke?"

Cops and Robbers, Good and Bad Guys

Murdoch ends up in the apartment of a hooker, where he reviews his wallet's contents. On seeing a picture of Emma, he wonders aloud whether he knows her or not. And he finds his driver's license, which indicates that his name is "John" which the hooker chuckles, "Well, that's an appropriate name."

Murdoch warns the hooker that these are dangerous times, especially for women in her line of work, as he exits her apartment. Still fascinated with Shell Beach, Murdoch sees a billboard for the vacation spot high on a building up the street. He decides to investigate more closely.

Up on the scaffolding under the billboard, Murdoch examines numerous press clippings about a murderer who's been stalking the city's street walkers. Murdoch is overcome by this information, as these clips apparently lead him to believe that he is, in fact, the killer.

In this moment, the shadowy figures who've been looking for him join him on the scaffolding. The leader of the group, Mr. Hand (played by Richard O'Brien), shocks Murdoch with this greeting: "So, it seems you've discovered your unpleasant nature."

On the surface, this seems like a statement simply about Murdoch's revelation that he is apparently the murderer that has the city in a panic. However, there could be another, deeper psycho-spiritual point that Proyas is making. Stripped raw, the human ego is at root motivated by the notion of kill-or-be-killed. Stuck in world of lack and "never enough," the ego personality feeds its "needs" by accumulating things, or even by killing if necessary to get what it wants. Only the rules of civil society stop the ego – our lower self – from doing whatever it takes to get what it believes it needs.

These Strangers are in hot pursuit of Murdoch, having followed him from the hotel room to this point high above this dark city. Murdoch is shocked by their appearance, asking them the obvious question: "Who are you?" Mr. Hand responds, "We might ask the same question, yes?"

Could Proyas be nodding again to Ramana Maharshi's most insightful question: "Who am I?"

"This Jesus Must Die"

Like he did to the clerk in the hotel room, Mr. Hand attempts to control Murdoch with his Jedi mind tricks, by saying "Sleep. Now." To Mr. Hand's surprise, Murdoch does not fall under this spell. Not only that, but as Murdoch makes the scaffolding collapse, the Strangers discover that Murdoch can "tune," which means that he has the gift of psychokinesis.

Proyas decides that now is a good time for us to really get to know who The Strangers are. We have found in the previous scene that they are not human. When a Stranger's head is sliced open in the confrontation on the scaffolding, a crab-like creature is revealed that had animated a dead human body. Now, as we descend into their subterranean lair, The Strangers are assembled in a theater-like configuration. One Stranger introduces the scene, "What is to be done? This man is dangerous."

This scene is reminiscent of a song from the musical *Jesus Christ Superstar*. In that song, the council of Pharisees decide that "He [Jesus] is dangerous," and conclude, "This Jesus must die."

This council of Strangers is told that sometimes humans can "tune," as Murdoch can. The explanation is that the "imprinting" sometimes doesn't "take," and that, consequently, "They behave erratically when they waken." Usually, these failed imprintees wander about like "lost children," but that Murdoch is different.

Next, Murdoch finds his way to "his" apartment that he apparently shares with Emma. As he sees her there, he expresses his skepticism about the whole situation, and asks her: "You're supposed to be my wife?"

Emma then proceeds to tell him about her conversation with the doctor who said that he had some kind of psychotic break and he feels that it is imperative that Murdoch see him.

"What happened to me?" Murdoch responds. "Why was I seeing a doctor?"

She has a whole story that explains her affair which upset him, and now he's being sought by the police, a suspect in the series of street-walker murders. He concludes: "Maybe I have lost my mind, but whoever I am, I'm still me, and I am not a killer." Even though he doesn't know his identity or his past history, he digs deep and knows that he's not a murderer.

Born Innocent

Proyas illustrates a profound spiritual point with the previous line. On the surface, even though Murdoch seems to have amnesia, he is also reflective, discovering his true essence is good. Metaphysically speaking, we could even say that Murdoch is recognizing that the illusionary Maya that he seems trapped in – this Plato's Cave – does not change the fact that his Higher Self is without sin or guilt. *(See Appendix A for more on Plato's Cave.)*

Bumstead (predictably) stakes out Murdoch's apartment, and attempts to apprehend John as he exits. Murdoch begins to explain that he is innocent, but stops, saying, "Yeah, who's gonna listen to a mad man?" Emma, the dutiful wife, aids John in his escape, throwing herself between Bumstead and Murdoch.

The inspector shrugs Emma off, and again reiterates his deeper, subterranean attitude, i.e., victim. He bemoans, "No one ever listens to me." The chase resumes, and Murdoch performs another miracle. What was once a solid wall now becomes a door. Unlike his last psychokinetic feat in the Automat, this one happens spontaneously, without Murdoch applying his will to it. The door just appears, with Murdoch having turned his back to the wall.

More Miracles

If you watch this scene closely, as Murdoch turns away from the wall, the same energy wave that he used to open the Automat door emanates from his head. In this case, however, it seems to happen spontaneously and effortlessly. Murdoch exits the building through this door, making his escape down an alley...from the darkness toward the light.

This doesn't feel like random filmmaking. Proyas is showing us what an awakening soul like Murdoch's might look like, how miracles just seem to unfold before him, with no effort, as he stumbles out of the darkness toward the light, both literally and spiritually.

By the time Bumstead gets to the wall/door through which Murdoch exited, the door is gone. It's just a wall again. However, Murdoch leaves a major clue for Bumstead – he dropped Dr. Schreber's card, the one Emma gave Murdoch back in their apartment.

Murdoch jumps in a cab where he sees a snow globe of Shell Beach on the dashboard, and asks the cabbie: "Do you happen to know the way to Shell Beach?" Despite the fact that the driver reports that he had honeymooned there, he can't seem to recall how to get to that idyllic place. (More on the symbolism of the elusive Shell Beach later.)

Shrinks are No Help

Dark City's storyline now focuses on Dr. Schreber. Bumstead initially meets up with him, in an elevator going down. The inspector expresses his skepticism to Dr. Schreber that Murdoch could be a murderer. Bumstead explains that he has come across quite a few murderers in his career, but that "Murdoch didn't strike him as one."

Early on in *Dark City*, Proyas establishes Bumstead's intensity and attention to detail. In one instance, he paused a moment to tell a uniformed policeman that his "shoelace is untied," this small thing was very noticeable to Bumstead.

In this brief encounter, Schreber gives a lightning-quick assessment of the detective's personality, noting that Bumstead is "fastidious man – driven – consumed by details." *Dark City* has started to dive deeper into the inner workings of the character's minds, symbolized by the descending elevator. Proyas is again providing us with a contrast between the intuitive Murdoch and the analytical Bumstead *vis-à-vis* the delivery system of a psychiatrist, Schreber.

As Schreber says to Bumstead, "Perhaps you are not accustomed to digging deep enough" into the workings of the human mind. Proyas is playing out the age-old ontological/deontological argument, where seemingly "scientific" analytical tools miss the big picture. Details may be useful, but they don't represent the whole, only the parts.

The Stranger called Mr. Hand tracks Schreber down at a public indoor pool. Mr. Hand reveals that The Strangers find water (he derisively calls it "moisture") uncomfortable. Again, the symbolism here is rich. Water – like light – is often a symbol for life. These Strangers have an aversion to both light and water for they are, in a sense, anti-life.

As Mr. Hand paces around the pool, he reprimands Schreber. The doctor begins to panic, splashing about in the pool now, in stark contrast to his near-comatose state by the edge of the pool just moments before. His excuse to Mr. Hand for not reporting in to The Strangers is, "I was frightened" and that "I have a weak heart." The dark-shrouded Strangers have been positioned by Proyas as victimizing authority figures.

A fun analogy would be to categorize Schreber as the Cowardly Lion figure from *The Wizard of Oz*. Bumstead, being all in his head would be the Tin Man, lacking a heart. And Walenski, cognitively struggling as he does through most of *Dark City*, fills the role of the Scarecrow. The wide-eyed, innocent Murdoch would fill the place of Dorothy. One of The Strangers whom we meet later – Mr. Book (played by Ian Richardson) – would be the closest analog to the Wizard himself in *Dark City*. Mr. Hand, with all his cruelty, resembles the Wicked Witch of the West. And finally, Shell Beach has similarities to the Emerald City of Oz.

Mr. Hand shows Schreber the broken syringe that they found in Murdoch's hotel room. The doctor explains in a panic that Murdoch "woke up and knocked the syringe right out of my hand." The fact alone that he woke up is a foreshadowing of him being exceptional.

Murdoch seems to have only fragments of memories (and certainly no memory of killing anyone). This turn of events seems to be because Schreber did not get a chance to inject Murdoch with this syringe. But, by not doing so, this enabled something to happen that made Murdoch extraordinary, helping him to take his seedling abilities to the next level. Much to Mr. Hand's chagrin, he tells Schreber that Murdoch can "tune." It seems that this is the point where it dawns on Dr. Schreber that things can change in this unnamed dark city, and that Murdoch is the key.

Toward the end of the Hand/Schreber encounter, Murdoch slips into the locker room just outside the pool. He hears bits and pieces of this conversation, as he examines Schreber's syringes. Not knowing whose side the doctor is on, Murdoch throws him off balance as Schreber tries to get out of the pool and finds the ladder is no longer there. Murdoch has once again used his psychokinetic ability to "move" the ladder to the other end of the pool, to Schreber's frustration and surprise.

Walenski: Enlightenment Breaking Bad

Bumstead later goes to Walenski's apartment and is greeted by his wife. Leading Bumstead to her husband's study, she expresses her deep concerns about him. As they enter the room, we see that Walenski's mania is in full bloom.

Walenski's study is not dissimilar to those made by the John Walsh character in *A Beautiful Mind*, who converted his garage into a kind of crazy man's lair. Spirals and press clippings populate Walenski's walls. He briefly acknowledges Bumstead but quickly returns to his wall scribbles. Walenski tells the inspector that he has been riding the subway in circles, looking for answers.

When Bumstead notes that his wife is concerned about him, Walenski asserts: "She's not my wife! I don't know who she is. I don't know who any of us are."

Walenski goes on: "Do you think about the past much, Frank?"

Bumstead responds: "As much as the next guy."

Now, Walenski becomes less of the delusional paranoid, and more the Indian sage: "See, I've been trying to remember things – clearly remember things – from my past, but the more I try to think back, the more it all starts to unravel. Nothing seems real. I've just been dreaming this life. When I finally wake up, I'll be somebody else, somebody totally different."

This is giving us an insight into what is happening in *Dark City*; Ed Walenski is beginning to solve the mystery. Bumstead – ever the detective – asks if Eddie "saw something," presumably something that would help Bumstead solve the case.

Walenski cries out, "There is no case! There never was! It's all just a big joke! It's a joke!"

The screenwriters (Proyas, Lem Dobbs and David S. Goyer) may or may not have intended it, but here Walenski seems to channel Ramana Maharshi at his most emphatic. The sage has said that the material world is governed by "leela," where things often make no sense, unless they are viewed as a divine comedy.

As Hindupedia puts it:

> Leela means an act, play.

> Example 1 - The cosmic sport is divine Leela. The struggle of creatures across the cycle of life and death, the veil of ignorance, realization and transcendence, all this forms a part of that Leela. It is called Leela in the sense that it passes over the subtle body of beings without making a difference to the actual state of existence of either the self or Brahman.

Dark City attempts to use words and images to explain the non-dual concept. Just as *The Matrix* taught us, "There is no spoon," Walenski is telling us, "There is no case." All the world is a stage, a play, a joke that seems to unfold before our eyes.

From a non-dual perspective, we see that Walenski is correct, but from Bumstead's perspective, he can't help but conclude that Walenski has careened into full-blown delusional paranoia.

Walenski and Murdoch eventually meet in a subway station later on in the storyline, apparently coincidentally. Walenski recognizes that Murdoch is at once a suspect but also a person who is also outside of The Stranger's grasp. Walenski is a beaten man, stating that "there's no way out, you know."

Wapnick's essay, "Our Gratitude to God," puts a finer point on this "no way out" notion:

> "There is a wonderful parable in Kafka's book, *The Trial*, which is basically a book about hopelessness and despair – there is no hope anywhere. Kafka presents a tale about a man who stands before the Law, and he is there for a whole lifetime. He is waiting for the man standing in front of the door, like a clerk, to let him go through the open door. He waits and waits and gets older and older; his voice becomes more and more feeble. Finally the man is almost dead and he says to the man in front of the door, "What is going to happen?" The reply is, "Well, this door was just for you, and now I am going to close it." And that's it – the end of the story! It is not very happy, but Kafka wasn't a happy man. He understood well, on some deep level, the absolute hopelessness and despair of the ego system, but

without knowing that there is a way out. There is no way out *within the system*! The ego tells us there is a door back to God, but we are never going to get to it, and finally that door is going to close. So there is nothing more than this ego thought system."[3]

Like Neo learned in *The Matrix*, there is no way out within the Matrix. The way out is to *transcend* the system.

Walenski describes to Murdoch what The Strangers have been doing, how they move things and people's memories all around, creating profound levels of confusion among the residents. Murdoch asks how Walenski knows all this, and he responds: "Once in a while, one of us wakes up while they are changing things. It's not supposed to happen, but it does. It happened to me."

Later in the scene, he reveals that he has figured out the ultimate way out. Unable to cope, Walenski decides to commit suicide, throwing himself in front of a subway car.

"You Can't Handle the Truth"
Walenski represents the downside to the quest for truth. One-pointed focus is often cited as the optimal path for seekers, but – like Jack Nicholson's character Col. Nathan R. Jessup in *A Few Good Men* – except for the very strongest among us, "you can't handle the truth" is itself a true statement.

According to many non-dual spiritual philosophies, what is widely accepted as common knowledge is in fact incorrect. The world is woefully mistaken about just about everything, but the awakening mind is especially vulnerable to spinning out into an apparent deranged state. Once unmoored from conventional "wisdom," the heretofore "blind" who are just beginning to see, still can't, in a sense, handle the truth.

This is a vitally important metaphysical insight. Even as we all know the Truth, we are all so scattered and confused, we don't know how to even begin to separate the wheat of truth from the chaff of lies. The ancient melody of love is always in our hearts, but we have all spent a lifetime covering over that love with a raft of fears, not even knowing which end is up!

Interestingly, Murdoch – as a more gentle personality than Walenski's – seemed better able to exit from the proverbial Plato's Cave with his sanity intact. We have the sense that while Walenski was waking up from the dreamstate, the energy reflected in his aggressiveness may have had something to do with his psychotic break and ultimate suicide. He could not handle the truth.

The point is made here that we as human beings become dependent on our assumptions about the world, and if those assumptions are exploded and replaced with nothing, is it any surprise that that void would create profound confusion, possibly leading to an overwhelming sense of panic?

This deep-seated confusion that is the human condition is not only a confusion about who we really are, but also a profound sense (if sublimated) of alienation and separation from those around us. Murdoch is like a lone wolf wandering the forest in search of an elusive goal for the first two-thirds of *Dark City*, only gaining his bearings in the latter part of the film.

Again, we could make an interesting case for viewing Murdoch in this movie as a Jesus figure, awake among sleepwalkers, where Detective Walenski is akin to a John the Baptist figure. So as John the Baptist preceded Jesus, Walenski precedes Murdoch. Unlike Jesus' "prince of peace" approach, John the Baptist was a voice in the wilderness with an almost demonic style, according to many Bible scholars. While it takes Murdoch some time to become a powerful, enlightened figure, he eventually transcends his confusion about who he is, in truth.

Walenski, like John the Baptist, also makes strides to wake from the pall that is life in this dark city. However, rather than transcend the insanity, Walenski is a wild man who wallows in his predicament, seeing no way out and overwhelmed by the enormous lie that he and his fellow citizens are living.

Contrast Walenski with Bumstead. Bumstead is – like virtually everyone else in *Dark City* – in a state of profound denial, and yet in many ways that denial works for Bumstead. He may have bought into the world being real, despite the obvious signs that something is very off in this town. Bumstead, like all but a few inhabitants, is so effectively "drugged up" that he doesn't notice that there's no daylight.

Murdoch's entry into Bumstead's orbit, however, was in many ways the best thing that could have happened to the inspector. As Murdoch peels away the illusions that are like the layers of an onion that The Strangers have created, Bumstead's eyes begin to see what was always available to him, i.e., that this dark city is a fabrication.

Murdoch's Search Continues

As *Dark City*'s storyline turns back to Schreber, he limps back to The Stranger's underground command post, where we will discover how The Strangers manipulate the memories of the residents of this dark city. As Strangers pick and choose "memories" from a conveyor belt, we see Dr. Schreber working, mixing concoctions including "a touch of unhappy childhood, a dash of teenage rebellion, and last but not least a tragic death in the family."

The lead Stranger, Mr. Book, comes in and violently interrogates Dr. Schreiber as to why Murdoch is immune to their tuning. The goal of the Strangers is revealed as Dr. Schreber says that he does not know about the tuning, but it ultimately doesn't matter since what they are looking for is the human soul. Dr. Schreber continues, "That's the purpose of your little zoo, isn't it? That's why you keeping changing people and things around every night. Maybe you finally found what you were looking for and it's going to bite you on your...."

"Shut It Down!"

Next, we see The Strangers assemble in their Great Hall. Mr. Book intones: "Shut it down!" at the stroke of midnight. We see assorted vignettes of the citizenry going about their humdrum lives, but they all stop dead in their tracks, falling asleep.

We see a series of events in the world grind to a halt: a train stops, all cars stop because their drivers are asleep, etc. One cute aside that Proyas shows us is a movie marquee, with the words reading "now showing," *The Evil*, and then next to it "coming attractions," telling us the next film showing will be *Book of Dreams*. While it's easy to dismiss The Strangers as being "evil," especially at this stage in *Dark City*, by this marquee, Proyas is reminding us that what's unfolding on the screen is but a dream, thus far a nightmarish one.

Of course, the one resident of this dark city who doesn't fall asleep this time is Murdoch. Above ground, he seems disturbed by all his fellow citizens falling asleep when The Strangers have shut it down, so he implores them to "wake up" in escalating tones. Exasperated, he finally shouts, "Can anybody hear me?!"

And, yet, they all remain quite asleep. Proyas shows us how a spiritually awakening soul might feel surrounded by the spiritually asleep.

One of the most psycho-spiritually interesting sequences in *Dark City* involves a working-class couple complaining about their lot in life, seated at a grim dinner table. At the stroke of midnight, they fall asleep, along with everyone else.

Schreber imprints the couple with new personas, that of a wealthy couple. Their dingy apartment is transformed into a grand townhouse. Their tiny dinette set expands into a long and elegant dining room table. Their shabby clothes are exchanged for formal attire.

And, yet, when they awaken and resume their conversation, they continue to complain and whine. While the issues at hand change, the underlying discontent remains unaltered.

Talk about a masterful illustration by Proyas about the human condition! This same couple will find something about their material circumstances to complain about, at any socioeconomic strata. Proyas – of Greek parents, born in Egypt but raised in Australia – shows us that discontent and suffering are inward conditions that have little to do with one's life situation.

During this sequence, Murdoch finally meets Dr. Schreber, who is also awake. Murdoch is at his wit's end, grilling Schreber about why everyone's asleep and "why are they trying to kill me?" In another spontaneous energy burst from Murdoch, Schreber is flung many yards down the street. Both are stunned by Murdoch's ability. Schreber excitedly explains that Murdoch has their power. "You can make things happen by will alone," Schreber says.

Schreber proposes that he and Murdoch work together to "take this city back" from The Strangers. However, in that moment, several Strangers approach, and Murdoch scurries away. We then see the residents of this dark city re-awaken, once again going about their business.

Permanent Nightfall

There is another interesting nightclub scene where Emma sings a song called, "The Night Has a Thousand Eyes." Proyas deepens the psycho-spiritual themes in *Dark City* by this song's lyrics:

> 'cause the night has a thousand eyes
> And a thousand eyes will see me too
> And no matter what I do
> I could never disguise all my little white lies
> 'cause the night has a thousand eyes

Beneath our civilized world, these lyrics point to the human condition as being one of tremendous guilt. We believe that our disguise – our personas – that we have tried to cover over and hide even from ourselves are really just easily-seen-through lies. This cycle of sin, guilt, and fear is what makes the world go 'round, at least apparently so for those of us who are asleep and don't know it. An awakening soul like John Murdoch challenges that premise, and by his example can potentially rouse us from our sleep as well.

(Aside: In the theatrical release of Dark City, Connelly's vocals were dubbed over. In the director's cut, however, the vocals are sung by Connelly herself. Her voice is lovely.)

If You Can't Beat 'em...

In The Strangers lair, we learn that Murdoch has become so much like The Strangers that Mr. Hand asserts: "So we must become like him." It is interesting that Murdoch has gained *their* abilities but they want to become like him, instead of wanting him to join them.

Schreber has concocted a new vial that he calls, "The Life and Times of John Murdoch, Volume Two." Mr. Hand and Schreber propose that Hand be injected with all Murdoch's memories as a means to counter Murdoch's newfound power.

Some of The Strangers object, but Mr. Book persuades the collective by emphatically stating that Mr. Hand is willing to "sacrifice for the greater good." Perhaps heavy-handedly, Mr. Hand is strapped to a kind of crucifix in preparation for the "imprinting," where Schreber imprints this Stranger with Murdoch's memories.

After the injection, Mr. Book asks Mr. Hand whether the imprinting took. "Oh, yes, Mr. Book," says Mr. Hand, "I have John Murdoch...in mind."

Interesting word choice, that. That term would normally be used as another way to say, "I am thinking about John Murdoch." In this scene we are led to believe that he has *the thoughts of* John Murdoch. Mr. Hand now has access to two sets of memories and thought patterns, his own and Murdoch's.

This begins to explore interesting epistemic ground. Is an individual's consciousness simply a function of the brain, which stores information and learns the cognitive skills to think and analyze? Or is the brain more like what Nicola Tesla called a "receiver" (or a radio tuner!) that gathers knowledge from the collective unconscious, bringing it forward into time and space?

Many have posited, for example, that "inspiration" is not simply a function of the brain. Great works of art and music, for instance, reportedly "come from somewhere else." The artist often feels more like a "channel" than a "creator."

Proyas doesn't offer a definitive stance on where mind and thought come from, but he has set up *Dark City* as a playground for us to experiment with these ideas.

Home Is Where the Heart Is

Mr. Hand is now on an intensified search for Murdoch. Equipped with Murdoch's memories, Mr. Hand now recalls a special waterfront place where Emma and John met. There, Mr. Hand finds Emma, contemplatively gazing into the distance.

Mr. Hand initiates conversation with Emma. He opens by saying how "lucky" we are to be able to visit special places from our past "that meant so very much to us."

Emma counters, "I thought it was more that we were haunted by them."

Again, psycho-spiritual insight drips in this interchange. Sentimentality seems important and special to us, whereas painful memories are things we attempt to suppress in our psyches. But this judging of the positive and the negative from our pasts is what keeps the entire ego facade going. We attempt to blot out the pain by covering it over with the pleasant. This sublimation strategy seems to work in the short term, but many psycho-spiritual thinkers suggest that it is but a patch, one that only delays the pain for another day, while it festers beneath the surface.

As that tormented Shakespearean soul Hamlet began to understand, "...there is nothing either good or bad, but thinking makes it so. To me it is a prison." Positive or negative life situations are artificial labels, for life is just life, neither good nor bad. It is the investment in this up-and-down drama that imprisons us emotionally and spiritually.

Mr. Hand goes deeper. "Imagine a life," he says, "alien to yours, in which your memories were not your own, but those shared by every other of your kind. Imagine the torment of such an existence. No experiences to call your own."

Emma plays along: "If it was all you knew, maybe it would be a comfort."

"But if you were to discover something different, something better...," Mr. Hand trails off. Having Murdoch's memories – a human's recollections – seems to be that "something better," but this can also be construed as what is described in Western traditions as the original-sin myth. Once, we were one with God, but we fell from grace. We became individuals, which, for a moment, at least, felt "better."

As the theory goes, being autonomous from God has a certain excitement about it, and yet it is at the same time quite uncomfortable. We are not "at home." We are not with our Creator. It's no surprise, then, that we are thought to live bipolar existences that Shakespeare's Macbeth describes oh so well:

> Life's but a walking shadow, a poor player
> That struts and frets his hour upon the stage
> And then is heard no more: it is a tale
> Told by an idiot, full of sound and fury,
> Signifying nothing.

In the meantime, Murdoch meets up with his Uncle Karl, whom he's not seen in years. Karl treats Murdoch to a slideshow of Johnny's childhood spent at Shell Beach. We learn how Murdoch grew up. Of course, when Murdoch asks Karl how to get to Shell Beach, his uncle cannot recall.

Proyas's rendition of Shell Beach as "Home" could be symbolic of man's search for Heaven. Having everyone remembering glimpses but never totally recalling how to get there is like us having fallen from grace. However, part of us – sometimes called our Higher Self – wants to return Home to God. The ego, or lower self, on the other hand, wants nothing of this God and Heaven stuff, but strives to keep our Higher Self dormant, asleep to maintain the status quo.

Carrying this mythology into *Dark City*, we begin to understand why no one can tell Murdoch how to get to Shell Beach. The sleepwalking residents of this dark city vaguely know of Shell Beach; some even faintly recalling having been there. Many whom Murdoch asks for directions at first reply that it's easy to get to, and yet when pressed have no idea how to get to Shell Beach.

The slideshow continues. Karl reveals that Murdoch's parents died in a fire that little Johnny survived. And yet Murdoch finds an inconsistency: while the fire visibly scarred his arm as a youth, as an adult now, there is no scar! He presents this to Uncle Karl, who feebly asks, "What does it mean, Johnny?"

Lies, Lies, and More Lies

Murdoch sweeps all the slides off the table, exclaiming: "It means these are all lies!"

The past is past. The past is gone. The past never was. Many Eastern spiritualities suggest that liberation from suffering requires that we recognize that our memories are highly suspect, shot through with remembrances that are at best distortions of a series of events. The past seemed to have happened, but while we can review past events with our spotty memories, according to Eastern traditions, our past is a lie, a fabrication. To live in the past is to live in a prison.

Proyas bangs home this theme of "the past is a lie" when Emma and Bumstead discover that yet another call girl has been murdered. Turns out, she was actually killed by The Strangers, but of course Bumstead and Emma know nothing of The Strangers. She's dejected, thinking at this point that her husband is indeed the man who is committing these murders.

Before driving off, she notices Bumstead's accordion in the back seat. The young woman comments on its beauty. Recall, however, that the accordion, with its black-and-white keys, was theorized to symbolize the yin-and-yang concept from the Taoist tradition.

Bumstead muses that the accordion was a gift from his mother, but that – inexplicably – he can't recall when she gave it to him. He questions his memory, and wonders how he could possibly forget such an event. Bumstead is beginning to question his reality. And then he asks her: "Do you think about the past much, Mrs. Murdoch?"

Emma, rather than answer the question, simply responds with another question, "What's happening, Inspector?"

"I'm not sure I know any more," he replies.

Dazed and Confused

This marks a significant turning point in the movie, despite the exchange seeming to be a mere aside. Both Bumstead and Emma are now starting to question the reality that they both seem to be living out. That which appeared real seems to be questionable, although neither Bumstead nor Emma are not yet in the neighborhood of truth.

Cut back to Murdoch and Karl. Now, Murdoch notices that time itself seems warped. It seems to be nighttime, but he asks, "What happened to the day? How did I miss it?"

Aside from Uncle Karl's slides of his childhood (which were all lies!), Murdoch now notices that it's always been dark since he woke in the bathtub. This makes no sense to him; he is in full-blown skepticism about all that he perceives.

He retires to his childhood bedroom. There he again looks at some more pictures of his family, and then picks up an old scrapbook, which is titled with a child's penmanship, "Guide to Shell Beach, by Johnny Murdoch." The pages, however, are all empty.

Mr. Hand next has a moment of inspiration in which the Murdoch-in-his-mind (correctly) suggests that John is visiting Uncle Karl. The Stranger tracks Murdoch down at Karl's place, and a knife fight ensues, with Murdoch getting the better of Mr. Hand. With a hand to Mr. Hand's throat and a knife pointed at his head, Murdoch gets this Stranger to reveal what's going on here in this dark city.

Mr. Hand explains that the city is a great experiment, one which is reconstructed from human memories and experiences. It is purposely a hodge-podge of different styles of buildings from different eras, all designed to expose what makes humans tick. "Each night, we revise it, refine it," Mr. Hand says about Dark City, "in order to learn."

"Learn what?" asks Murdoch.

"About you, Mr. Murdoch," Mr. Hand replies. "You and your fellow inhabitants...what makes you human."

Mr. Hand explains that The Strangers "need to be like you."

With a burst of power, Mr. Hand pushes Murdoch off him, and the chase continues. In a nick of time, Bumstead and Emma pull up in a car, and Murdoch jumps in and they speed off.

The Third Degree

In the police interrogation room, Bumstead presses Murdoch with questions about the murders that Murdoch is suspected of committing. Murdoch turns the tables on Bumstead. He asks Bumstead if he has heard of and knows how to get to Shell Beach. Bumstead knows it, but, like the rest of the inhabitants of this dark city, the inspector can't quite seem to recall how to get there. "Don't you find that kind of odd?" asks Murdoch.

"I've got a better one for you," Murdoch continues, "When was the last time you remember doing something during the day?"

Again, Murdoch stumps Bumstead. Murdoch concludes that "the night never ends here."

"That's crazy," Bumstead responds flatly.

Murdoch agrees, "Damn right it's crazy."

It is at this seminal point that Bumstead's ideas about Murdoch change.

Dark City points to the psycho-spiritual perspective that the world is, in a sense, a vast insane asylum. Humans – with our limited ability to perceive "the big picture" – walk about with a series of erroneous assumptions about what "reality" is. Based on these false premises, we conjure up stories about what has and is going on in our experience.

Murdoch offers Bumstead a bold explanation for what's happening here: "It's not just me. It's all of us. They are doing something to all of us."

In isolation, this might sound like the ravings of a paranoid schizophrenic. But Bumstead can't help but see that something is "rotten in Denmark." And, yet, at the same time, the inspector finds Murdoch's explanation somewhat threatening. If time and space are being manipulated by The Strangers and if the residents of this dark city are all insane, it is understandable that Bumstead recoils from Murdoch's hypothesis. The very foundation of his thought system is being challenged.

"Shut up! I've heard enough," the inspector says, using the defense mechanism of denial to protect his psyche.

Shaken, Bumstead stands and walks over to the window. "There has to be an explanation for this," he says.

Murdoch then performs another miracle, psycho-kinetically levitating a book off the interrogation-room table. "Explain this," Murdoch says calmly, facetiously.

Never Assume

With the exception of John Murdoch, Schreber, and possibly Walenski, all the human players in *Dark City* are effectively hypnotized by their false memories. For everyone except these three, none of the thoughts

71

and memories that they have been injected with by The Strangers are in any way true.

One of the most powerful illustrations of non-dual metaphysics that *Dark City* offers is the idea that what we believe happened in time and space did not happen in reality. From a non-dual perspective, oneness is eternal; it is love, unchanging and unchangeable. Anything that is not this unchangeable love is, from this perspective, not real.

Extending this theory, memories can be modified and selective, and our personal story is one of continuous change. Therefore, our memories of our personal history, being chock full of qualities other than unchangeable love, are mere *fabrications,* stories that we (often wrongly) assume are true.

"You Can't Fake Something Like That"

The notion is paid off in the beautiful scene in the jail, where Emma visits Murdoch. She seems distraught, begging him for forgiveness for her (false memory of a) dalliance with another man.

Murdoch insists that she need not feel this way, that in fact, "I don't believe it ever happened." Emma counters that she can remember it all so vividly, but Murdoch assures her that she's mistaken. He suggests that her memories are false, and that their history together began just a day ago, rather than years ago.

"I remember falling in love with you," she says. "I love you, John. You can't fake something like that."

"No, you can't," he responds.

It is important to note that Murdoch doesn't comment on Emma's memory of falling in love. Instead, he only affirms the idea that love cannot be faked! We can assume that even though their roles have changed through The Strangers influence, they have nevertheless loved each other for a very long time.

Murdoch closes his eyes, focusing his mind. He presses his bound hands on the plate glass separating him and Emma, and this barrier shatters into millions of pieces. Their embrace in this touching scene reminds us that we are all deeply connected at a spiritual level.

Be Careful What You Wish For

With Murdoch in prison, *Dark City* now turns to Bumstead, who is conflicted about his success. While most would feel triumphant in such a moment as this, he is not. He has supposedly caught the serial killer, but we see him next somberly sitting at his desk looking at a Shell Beach post card. Also on his desk, we see – prominently – that same picture of his mother that we saw in his apartment when we first met Bumstead early in the film.

A uniformed officer enters his office, there to inform Bumstead that Inspector Walenski has committed suicide and that the chief of police wants to see Bumstead. The officer adds: "I knew you'd track the killer down, sir."

Bumstead can only muster a weak, "Hmmm." Head down, he glumly exits his office. Proyas is showing us that Bumstead is grappling not only with this case, but his very identity. This scene suggests that Bumstead could be thinking about things like: why he can't recall how to get to Shell Beach; how Murdoch could possibly have performed his levitation "trick"; why he can't remember the daylight; even why he can't remember when his mother gave him his accordion.

Aside from the rare individual, the sorts of thoughts that burden our daily lives are about grieving about the past and fretting about the future, never living in the present moment. Bumstead is coming to a crisis point.

Yes, something has clearly changed about Inspector Bumstead. The same officer that was chastised earlier for not having his shoelace tied, in passing, points out Bumstead's untied lace.

All of this indicates that he is beginning to question his reality and has started the process of shedding his persona, in this case, that of "fastidious, methodical, analytical, by-the-book public servant, covering over his tortured, aggrieved, wounded child."

Proyas implies here that Bumstead's exposure to Murdoch has started the spiritual awakening process.

The Truth Hurts
It will, after all, set us free...the truth, that is. These three main characters are now on a collision course for truth, as represented by their pursuit of Shell Beach. With gun in hand, Bumstead insists that the threesome of himself, Murdoch, and Schreber make the trek to Shell Beach. While they drive in that direction, Murdoch asks Bumstead "What do you hope to gain by helping me?"

"The truth," Bumstead responds plainly and surely.

Dr. Schreber claims to have been to Shell Beach. Emphatically, he exclaims like a young child that he does not want to go to Shell Beach, "You can't make me go there!" It is somewhat akin to being at the doorstep of the Truth, or Heaven, and not wanting to pass through. Fear and doubt rule Dr. Schreber here, as it does most of humanity.

Murdoch, with a stare, silences Dr. Schreber. The power of Murdoch's will is now in full bloom. He is the leader and wayshower, which none can doubt when in his presence.

Dr. Schreber represents a deeply conflicted psyche. While he has been a vital player in The Stranger's experimentation in ego dynamics, he also recognizes that spirit – which Murdoch represents – is the true, real, and virtuous way.

Row Your Boat
And, yet, as determined as Murdoch and Bumstead are to reach Shell Beach, the obstacles put in their path seem insurmountable. They reach the place where the bridge to Shell Beach is supposed to be, and yet inexplicably there is no bridge. Undaunted, they secure a row boat.

We all remember the nursery rhyme:

> Row, row, row your boat,
> Gently down the stream.
> Merrily, merrily, merrily, merrily,
> Life is but a dream.

This subject will come up again, but if we look at this song closer, we can see that it was like a spiritual seed planted in each of us as children. Life is not the apparent life stories that each of us seems to live through and take very seriously, but *Row Your Boat* offers us a more light-hearted approach to life as it is all a dream anyway. Like the goings on in *Dark City*, the lives we live could be viewed as dreams, fabrications.

This rowing boat may be a coincidence, or it might be a possibility that Proyas was alluding to this "row your boat" insight.

All Will Be Revealed
While the threesome of Murdoch, Bumstead, and Dr. Schreber row toward Shell Beach, Dr. Schreber tells them a story, one that starts out with overtones of Genesis 1:

> "First there was darkness. Then came The Strangers. They abducted us, and brought us here. This city – everyone in it – is their experiment. They mix and match our memories as they see fit, trying to divine what makes us unique. One day a man might be an inspector, the next someone entirely different. When they want to study a murderer, for instance, they simply imprint one of their citizens with a new personality – arrange a family for him, friends, an entire history. Even a lost wallet. Then they observe the results. Will a man, given the history of a killer, continue in that vein? Or are we in fact more than the mere sum of our memories. This business of you being a killer was an unhappy coincidence. You have had dozens of lives before now. You just happened to wake up while I was

imprinting you with this one." *(See Appendix D for more on this dialog.)*

The age-old question is being asked here, what makes us uniquely human beings? What are the defining qualities that make us tick; are we the "mere sum of our memories" or are we "more"?

Ever practical, Bumstead asks: "Why are they doing all this?"

Dr. Schreber goes on: "It is our capacity for individuality, our souls, that makes us different from them. They think they can find the human soul if they understand how our memories work. All they have are collective memories. They share one group mind. They're dying, you see. Their entire race is on the brink of extinction. They think we can save them."

Ever curious, Murdoch asks: "Where do I fit in?"

"You are different, John," Dr. Schreber responds. "You resisted my attempt to imprint you."

He explains further that Murdoch has developed the same ability to tune that The Strangers have. They've buried machines deep below the city that helps them to focus their telepathic energies, and Murdoch has tapped into that power.

The reason The Strangers are using Dr. Schreber is that they needed his knowledge of the human psyche to manipulate individual memories as part of their experiments.

Murdoch becomes exasperated, wondering what happened to his past, his childhood.

"You still don't understand, John," Dr. Schreber says, plainly. "You were never a boy. Not in this place. Your entire history is an illusion, a fabrication, as it is with all of us!" It must be disconcerting to hear that you will never remember your childhood, your parents, or your past. That knowledge is irretrievably lost.

Bumstead asks Dr. Schreber where the citizens of this dark city came from. Unfortunately, the doctor does not recall, as he vaguely looks to the sky and says, "Somewhere else." He knows that all were abducted but has no recollection of Earth. In essence, the memories that have circulated around the populace are from a limited pool, there are no "real" personal memories to be had anymore.

Proyas sets this scene up as a kind of River Styx from Greek mythology, with these three leaving the underworld in a quest to return to Earth, to Home, in this case represented by Shell Beach. He seems to explicitly reiterate that the world they've been living in is a kind of a Grand Illusion. There's even a nod to the Buddhist and Hindu concept of reincarnation, as he suggests that Murdoch (and presumably all of them) have lived "dozens of lives."

Landing on the other side, these three discover that instead of finding the actual Shell Beach, they instead find only a weak replica of the place, a billboard. "There is no ocean, John," Dr. Schreber says. "There is nothing beyond this city. The only place home exists is in your head," he chuckles.

If a Tree Falls in a Forest...

The Alpha and the Omega, the beginning and the end of all things, arises and falls in consciousness. It is what the Buddhist koan, "If a tree falls in a forest and no one is around to hear it, does it make a sound?" is all about. The phenomenal world seems to be unfolding all around us, but until it is perceived by consciousness, the material world for all intents and purposes does not exist. Existence arises in awareness, is co-created with consciousness.

A metaphysical view of consciousness would be that the mind labels things: "ocean," "spoon," "good," "bad," etc. Prior to conscious thought, there is only the eternal, which some call "love," or "God," or "universe."

Murdoch, however, finds Dr. Schreber's explanation wanting. He begins to tear away at the paper billboard, exposing a solid brick wall. That's not enough for him. He finds a long-handled hammer and begins smashing through the brick wall. Bumstead follows suit, despite Dr. Schreber's protestations.

Break On Through to the Other Side

The two successfully break through, only to find that on the other side of the wall is empty space, a night sky.

The Strangers, led by Mr. Hand, enter from behind. Mr. Hand announces: "And now you know the truth." (Recall that finding the truth is Bumstead's announced intention.)

A fight ensues, and during the struggle, a Stranger and Bumstead fall outside the brick wall and into space. As we float along with Bumstead, the camera reveals that this dark city is a small planetoid, perhaps a large space station, surrounded by a thin atmospheric bubble.

Back inside, we see that Mr. Hand has brought along Emma, whom he holds at knife point. Mr. Hand threatens to kill her unless Murdoch surrenders, which he does to save her life.

The Strangers transport Murdoch to their underground chambers, where he is strapped to the round crucifix that Mr. Hand had been put on earlier. A Stranger examines Murdoch, finding that his fingerprints have a unique spiral pattern. "The doctor was right," the examining Stranger says, "he has evolved." The spiral could be a metaphysical pointer to a labyrinth, ever working inward to the peaceful center.

Crucifixion. Resurrection.

A chant of "kill him" arises among the assembled Strangers, again evoking "this Jesus must die."

Mr. Book, however, believes that Murdoch represents their Holy Grail, or salvation. Even as Mr. Book acknowledges that Murdoch is "powerful, yes, dangerous," he also represents their key to "the soul."

"It is time to be one with John Murdoch," Mr. Book intones. Which is an interesting twist on the religious goal of being "one with God." One could say that it is the ego who wants to become a "god," and believes that it has now found a way to do so.

Now that they have Murdoch, there is no need for the rest of the city's residents. "Shut it down," Mr. Book commands, "Shut it down forever!" This would also be an ego maneuver, self-centered and concerned only for itself alone.

Schreber is given a syringe, with the intention of imprinting Murdoch with the collective memories of The Strangers, making Murdoch one of them. However, recall that Murdoch had pocketed Dr. Schreber's syringe, the one with all the answers.

It turns out that Schreber's syringe carried a powerful punch! We get a glimpse into Murdoch's head, as Dr. Schreber has imprinted him with the secrets of The Strangers. This new imprinting includes memories that involve Murdoch learning the Jedi-type ways in a hyper-accelerated manner. We see flashbacks of a young Murdoch learning how to master his innate telekinetic powers. In short, he gets "a lifetime of knowledge in a single syringe." This is reminiscent of scenes from *The Matrix*, where the characters can download entire training programs, from flying a helicopter to learning karate.

Murdoch is instructed to take control of The Stranger's machine, the one that amplifies their thoughts and enables them to rearrange this dark city to their will on a daily basis. Dr. Schreber's marching orders at the end of this session are: "You have the power to make anything happen, but you must act now!"

A new, all-powerful Murdoch arises from his "cross." His restraints, and the entire contraption, simply melt away, as he stands tall to face The Strangers. He and Mr. Book standoff in a battle of wills. Both are capable of tremendous psychokinetic powers, and they grapple with their minds in a way that leads to severe devastation of the surrounding structures. The Stranger's chambers are laid to waste, and both Murdoch and Mr. Book ascend into the skies above the city where their fight continues. This is also similar to scenes from the later *Matrix* movies.

Of course, Murdoch wins this titanic battle, with Mr. Book's vessel of a body perishing, as his crab-like essence scurries away. Murdoch gently returns to ground, where he surveys the damages.

Phoenix from the Ashes

A proud Dr. Schreber greets Murdoch. He asks him, "What are you going to do now, John?"

"You told me I had the power, didn't you?" Murdoch replies matter-of-factly. He turns to the city, and with his mind, he begins the process of fixing the entire town, repairing it.

But his work is not done. Murdoch still must return home, to get back to Shell Beach. Along the way, Murdoch encounters Mr. Hand, who reports that he is dying. Having Murdoch's "imprint" in him does not agree with The Strangers and their alien constitutions. Still, Mr. Hand goes on, he did want "to know what it was like...how you feel."

Murdoch quickly corrects him: "You know how I was *supposed to* feel. That person isn't me. Never was."

"You wanted to know what it was about us that made us human," Murdoch continues. "Well, you're not going to find it...in here." He points to his head. "You went looking in the wrong place." Although it may seems cliché to some, he was indicating that a person's essence is in not in the head, but rather the heart.

Many spiritualities suggest that the intellect by its nature can lead us astray. Over the centuries, science has developed theories about the natural world that proved to be colossally incorrect. This is especially true about the nature of the human body, and even more so about what makes humans tick cognitively and psychologically.

The Strangers in *Dark City* serve as scientists. Their hypothesis is that humans are the sum total of their memories. This film implies that this hypothesis is simply incorrect, that memories have very little to do with who we are, although virtually all of us do allow our memories to rule us.

Murdoch turns and walks away. He shifts this little planet they occupy, and for the first time, the sun rises on this heretofore dark city. He opens the door of what has been a dungeon to reveal the sun, the ocean, and a pier. At the end of the pier stands Emma, who after her last imprinting, believes her name is Anna.

Murdoch walks to the end of the pier, where they engage in polite chit chat. Anna is radiant, smiling. Both exude a sense of innocence about them. He asks her where Shell Beach is. She points to it, saying she's headed that way, "would you like to join me?"

"Sure," he says, and they walk off together. When she asks him his name, he says simply, "John. John Murdoch."

Of course, that is *not* his name, but rather the last name that The Strangers gave him. In the moment, however, there seemed no need for this newly awakened person to give himself another name. "John Murdoch" will do just fine.

A new day has arisen and they – as well as all of the residents of this (formerly) dark city – will create new memories as they move onward through life.

Overcoming the Illusion

Some may not have taken to *Dark City*, with its *noir*-ish presentation and complex storyline. *Dark City* can be confusing, as it reflects John Murdoch's confusion, making it at times hard to follow. The film's special effects seem to be done awkwardly at times, and the editing and sound are sometimes clipped.

Nevertheless, the metaphysical and psycho-spiritual content of *Dark City* are unmistakable and wonderfully illustrated, without feeling pedantic or preachy.

Endnotes for *Dark City*

[1] Jay Dyer, "Dark City (1998) – Esoteric Analysis," Jay's Analysis, (2010) jaysanalysis.com/2010/10/12/1165/

[2] Eric G. Wilson, "Gnostic Paranoia in Proyas's Dark City" Literature/Film Quarterly, (2006), www.questia.com/read/1P3-1214287831/ gnostic-paranola-in-proyas-s-dark-city

[3] Kenneth Wapnick, Ph.D., "Our Gratitude to God," Foundation for A Course in Miracles, www.facim.org/online-learning-aids/excerpt-series/ our-gratitude-to-god/part-vii.aspx

Inception: **The dream is real**

Inception is – in many ways – one of the most ambitious films ever made, particularly among those that are so steeped in metaphysical content. Reality is called into question at the core in this film, and it's done so in an especially inventive way.

While the idea of a dream within a dream has been done previously, the world created by *Inception*'s writer/director Christopher Nolan (*Memento, Dark Knight*) is a filmic *tour de force*, one that deeply questions the universe – at its root. There are – in all – three levels of dream realities presented in the movie *Inception* (the van, hotel, and snow levels) with a bonus dreamscape known as Limbo.[1]

Perhaps even more powerfully, Nolan makes us question whether the "reality" that we live in is *itself* a dreamy illusion. As Mal (played by Marion Cotillard) – Dom Cobb's (played by Leonardo DiCaprio) wife – poignantly states: "You don't know you're dreaming." This rings true, since when we are dreaming, that fantasy world becomes our reality. While we are in it, we simply don't recognize it as a fabricated fantasy, for in the moment, the dream seems quite real.

Nolan has the reputation as an enigmatic filmmaker. Perhaps best known for his take on Batman with the *Dark Knight* trilogy, Nolan clearly has the ability to make esoteric, mind-bending flicks like *Memento*. *Inception* was, like so many Hollywood films, a long time in the making, taking 10 years from inception (pun intended) to completion. The British auteur is no mere stylist, for his command of deep psychological, metaphysical, and spiritual themes are artfully woven into the complex tapestry that he offers us in *Inception*.

While the business of Hollywood filmmaking can have incredibly high-stakes (often involving $100+ million budgets, as *Inception* had) Nolan has established himself as a "bankable" director, affording him great latitude in developing projects that he believes will entertain but also provoke thought. While Steven Spielberg can make a philosophically interesting film like *Minority Report*, he seems most in his wheelhouse when making more pop-oriented films like *Jurassic Park* and *Raiders of the Lost Ark*. Nolan seems more driven to push the envelope in his mainstream offerings, including his takes on the Batman franchise. Nolan generally writes what he directs, indicating that his interest in the deeper meaning of his work is, well, deep.

While *Inception* is structured as a heist flick, that is only about the *form*. The *content* is a study in applied epistemology, in which a theory of knowledge is both presented and illustrated. While the storyline is propelled by Saito (played by Ken Watanabe) hiring Dom Cobb to plant a thought in Robert Fischer's (played by Cillian Murphy) head, that's just on the surface. The more meaningful journey portrayed in the movie explores the workings of Cobb's mind, a man who'd experimented on the very essence of his wife Mal's consciousness, with disastrous results. While executing an inception appears to be "just a job," Nolan has presented us with a made-up scenario in film to illustrate how the mind functions.

A Theory of *Inception*: What Makes this Work Tick?

Films of a metaphysical or spiritual nature are often philosophically radical, meaning that they dive deep into – and bring to light – our most fundamental beliefs...about the world, our thoughts, and our relationship and interactions with the universe. Those movies with a more meditative – sometimes mystical – bent explore our core thought systems and the intricate nature of human consciousness.

On the surface, *Inception* is a very elaborate, highly engaging Hollywood movie, but it also masterfully traces how the two main characters cognitively arrive in the places of consciousness that they do. Again, on the surface, the film is about how a team of psychological spies (for lack of a better term) will plant the seed of a thought in Robert Fisher's head that will lead him to change his mind about how he will run his newly inherited business. Even as that is *Inception*'s storyline, the film is more about the thought system of Dom Cobb.

With both the Fischer and Cobb characters, we can observe how a belief about something is adopted at a point in one's life, and how that belief – even if it is untrue – can spin one's life out of control, leading to unpleasant outcomes. These belief systems are reinforced by experience, thereby weaving a tangled web of a life "story." If we apply these thoughts to our own lives, we may well find that, in the end, we have done the same and have based our life "story" on false premises and self-deception, and its end result has created what we might call our "personality" or our "identity."

While *Inception* is intriguing from start to finish, certain sequences of scenes seem most poignant and open to deconstruction. Several of note follow:

Parisian "Projections"

As *Inception* progresses, Cobb needs a dream architect for the work he does to complete the job. The architect serves the function of "dreamer of the dream," a concept of note that is used in the great spiritual work, *A Course in Miracles* (ACIM*)*.

As the gold standard of film websites, IMDb.com, puts it in its "FAQ for *Inception*":

"The terms Nolan uses in the film suggest he is drawing strongly on the metaphysics given in [ACIM]. This modern-day channeled text – purportedly from Jesus – has heavily influenced many current spiritual teachers, and counts Oprah Winfrey, Deepak Chopra, and Louise Hay amongst its fans. It suggests that we live in a dream reality peopled by projections of our own unconscious guilt, and have buried deep within our minds the truth that we are innocent, [and] only dreaming a dream of guilt, separation, and fear."[2]

Specifically, the late dean of ACIM scholars – Dr. Kenneth Wapnick – describes the "dreamer of the dream" in his essay, "The Happy Dream":

"'*You* are the dreamer of the world of dreams. No other cause it has, nor ever will.'[3]
"Note that the word 'you' is italicized: '*You* are the dreamer.' The you is the dreamer, not the dream figure. The dream figure is the person we think we are – the name we give ourselves, the bodies that we experience and perceive, etc. The you is the dreamer, the decision-making part of the mind. In other words, the world does not come from itself – the world is not its own beginning and its own ending. It is literally the projection of our mind – just as when we sleep at night, the dreams we have are literally the projections of our brains. They have no reality outside of that."[4]

The consciousness of the "architect" in *Inception* – functioning as the dream maker – fabricates the world and its doings.

Cobb's first architect, Nash (played by Lukas Haas), botches the extraction of information from Saito. Interestingly, even though Nash later sells Cobb out to Saito, and Saito offers Cobb a gun to shoot Nash to exact revenge, Cobb responds, "That's not how I deal with things." We learn that while Cobb is single-minded throughout the film – wanting only to reunite with his children – he is also not driven by vengeance. Even so, he declines an offer to work with Nash again. Vengeance may not be his thing, but he is nobody's fool, either.

Although Cobb is a skilled architect himself, he has enough self-honesty to recognize that he needs another architect. He therefore goes to Paris to meet with his father-in-law, Professor Miles (played by Michael Caine).

This passage in the script sets up an important theme in *Inception*:

COBB: If you have someone good enough, you have to let them decide for themselves. You know what I'm offering.

MILES: Money?

COBB: No, not just money: the chance to build cathedrals, entire cities – things that have never existed, things that couldn't exist in the real world...

Cobb recognizes that Truth cannot be thrust on a person. He or she needs to "decide for themselves." He also asserts that the intention to create, rather than simply acquiring money, is the more powerful motivator. Expanding the creative mind, engaging ourselves at our essence is what drives us, not just fulfilling baser materialistic "needs."

Taken together, this volitional pursuit of virtue becomes a metaphor for life, where we are presented with life lessons – ones we as individuals can choose to learn. Here is the potential for the end to suffering, to healing by transcending challenging situations. As Cobb says at one point, "The stronger the issues, the more powerful the catharsis."

Some believe that by exercising one's Higher Self – one's creative mind – one can break out of self-imposed boundaries, freeing oneself from the limitations of the everyday world. Dom Cobb does precisely this in *Inception*.

Alternatively, many a spirituality teaches that if a person resists what "is," he or she is often doomed to a life filled with anguish.

Although this Cobb/Miles dialog seems to only advance the storyline, its bigger purpose is to introduce the pivotal figure in *Inception* – Ariadne (played by Ellen Page). Although she is the youngest, least-experienced character in the film, Ariadne has a certain conflict-free purity of purpose and the gift of unadulterated (spiritual) vision. Cobb has mis-created in the past, using his creative skills in ways that – we later learn – have gone horribly wrong. Ariadne becomes critically important to the process of facilitating the righting of those wrongs.

After Cobb recruits Ariadne, he and Arthur begin to train her in the ways of dream manipulation. As a part of this process, Cobb has her create a street scene in Paris. As they begin to stroll down the boulevard, they have an engrossing, insightful interchange:

ARIADNE: Who are the people?

COBB: They're projections of my subconscious.

Wikipedia's description of psychological projection explains:

"Psychological projection was first conceptualized by Sigmund Freud as a defense mechanism in which a person unconsciously rejects his or her own unacceptable attributes by ascribing them to objects or persons in the outside world instead. Thus, projection involves psychically expelling one's negative qualities onto others, and is a common psychological process."

Quite the admission, then, by Cobb. Although in *Inception*, the Freudian notion of projection is taken to an esoteric level. All the people on the street in this scene are *entirely* Cobb's projections. It's not only the *attributes* and *attitudes* of the passersby that Cobb is projecting, it is their very *existence!*

Ariadne is not only dealing with the scene that she created, but she also, most importantly, has to learn how to create the construct to deal with all of the subject's unconscious projections. How that dreaming person fills in the blanks can lead to some nasty surprises.

A profound metaphysical concept is illustrated by the concept of projection: Oneness. In some Eastern spiritualities, specifically the Vedanta philosophy, as well as ACIM, the idea is that all of existence is one unified whole. It is only because of projection that we believe that the whole is divided into distinct parts, such as people, animals, and objects.

This oneness appears as many to Cobb and Ariadne, as it does for all of us. Our perception sees each "splinter" (person, place or thing) as unique and distinct from the other.

Cobb elaborates on how the process of projection works:

COBB: Sure – you are the dreamer, I am the subject. My subconscious populates your world. That's one way we get at a subject's thoughts – his mind creates the people, so we can literally talk to his subconscious.

To explain what Cobb has just told Ariadne, the dreamer of the dream experiences his or her reality by buying into the reality of this separated world that they have created. Doing so with the "subject's" subconscious creates a kind of veil of forgetfulness, where in this case Ariadne forgets her reality, replacing it with the subject's dream reality. The dream continues to subdivide with the help of the subject, and more splinters come to "life" – people she can now relate to *as if* they were real.

Now when it comes to *metaphysical* projection, the difference becomes even more pronounced than Freudian psychological projection. Freudian projection "dumps" unacceptable aspects of the self onto others, whereas the former literally creates an entire world from the mistaken view that the individual is separate from the whole, the oneness.

Nolan takes the dream world of *Inception* in even more radical directions now, giving it a mind-bending twist. Ariadne says:

> "I love the concrete sense of things. Real weight, you know? I thought a dream space would be all about the visual, but it's the feel of things. Question is, what happens as you start to mess with physics...."

This short paragraph has so much content! First, it is of note that she talks about the concrete sense of things. This is a marked reminder of the concept of lucid dreaming, where the dreamer knows that they are in a dream but still are fully engaged in the surrounding dreamscape. One thing about lucid dreaming that is not really emphasized is that even though the dreamer *knows* that he or she is dreaming, they still have all the body sensations of weight, touch, and sight, just as if they were physically there. This in itself gives credence to the idea that even though we feel as if we are having a physical experience in the world, it is actually something that is only going on in the mind.

As she's the creator of this dreamspace, Ariadne now performs what is, in this context, a miracle. With her mind, she turns the world over, bending the city of Paris upside down. This seems incredible, and yet from a metaphysical perspective, if Buddha could perform his "twin miracle" (producing flames from his upper body while streaming water from his lower body), why couldn't Ariadne bend Paris to her will? This created world, after all, is hers, and she is the Alpha and Omega!

Nolan then brings projection back toward the psychological versus the metaphysical. Ariadne begins to notice that the projected people they pass on the street seem to be getting hostile toward her.

ARIADNE: Why are they looking at me?

COBB: Because you're changing things. My subconscious feels that someone else is creating the world. The more you change things, the quicker the projections converge on you.

Change is sometimes threatening to the subconscious, which can be pessimistic about the future at worst, and resistant to change at best. It brings to mind people who are "control freaks" and "perfectionists." This can explain their behavior, as they would be filled with dread due to their underlying fear of change, and would struggle to maintain the status quo as a means to avoid the imagined tragic outcomes of the future.

Like most of the dream sequences in *Inception*, this one ends badly. Cobb's subconscious becomes confused as this dreamscape has elements of real things from his past, which in turn jeopardizes the lesson. Ariadne figures this out and confronts him.

> ARIADNE: You won't build yourself because if you know the maze, then she knows it. And she'd sabotage the operation. You can't keep her out, can you?

The "her" in this case is Cobb's late wife, Mal. Some have noted that it's probably short for "Mallory," a name which means something like "unfortunate." Of course, the prefix "mal" means something like "bad" or "evil," as in "malevolent" or "maladjusted." It is true that Mal's life was filled with misfortune, and now in death, she haunts Cobb's dreams. When she appears in *Inception*, she often does hurtful, vicious things, such as: stabbing Ariadne, shooting Arthur, as well as shooting Fischer in an attempted murder. Remember, though, that these events haven't really happened because she is only a dream figure that has been made "real" by Cobb's guilty mind. She is there as a representation of his guilt that he must eventually face, and will torment him and the others until he does so.

Ariadne strongly suggests that Cobb should disclose to the others his inability to get Mal out of his dreams, but he deflects. This is Cobb's deep, dark secret, something that consumes his inner world. On the surface, Cobb comes across as the archetypal "man in charge." Underneath, he is a roiling sea of conflict.

Her curiosity piqued, Ariadne cues into Cobb's dreaming mind and finds herself on an elevator, the same elevator that has brought Cobb down to his subterranean consciousness. Clearly she doesn't know what it's all about, but down she goes, unsure of what she'll find.

Nolan sets things up nicely throughout *Inception*, and this sequence of scenes is an excellent example. As this film begins, Cobb's task is to get secrets that are stored in a safe. Now, it's Ariadne turn to encounter a safe in this subterranean dreamscape. This is a great metaphor for the secrets that we hide even from ourselves. Only he knows the combination, and hopefully one day he (and we) will be brave enough to confront the terrors and guilt that has been locked away. She can't open it but her attention turns to a noise across the hall. It's Cobb and Mal, having a conversation in the living room.

When Cobb sees that Ariadne has entered what is in effect *his* dreamscape, he comes to her, saying that she "shouldn't be in here."

Ariadne then figures out that these are Cobb's *memories,* and that is why he had implored *her* not to use her actual memories in her work as an architect.

Ariadne anxiously points out that Cobb's guilty mind can't let Mal go. Tellingly, he responds:

> COBB: No. These are moments I regret. Moments I turned into dreams so I could change them.

Nolan has Cobb present quite the metaphysical perspective by saying that all memories are dreams, even though it proves to be impossible to change them because most believe that they have happened and are therefore cast in stone. Actually, our memories of past events are selective, spotty, and – most importantly – about non-eternal, temporal events that most think happened but are ultimately unreal. It may be hard to accept, but even *within* our memories of things past, we simply don't have a complete picture of what we believe we experienced. We instead have only selective memories about tiny slices of perceptions that we believe had happened in the past. Nothing more and nothing less.

Cobb has gone down the elevator many a time, frequently revisiting his guilt in hopes that he could somehow find a different outcome or another way to view what happened with Mal. He has never found a solution because, in essence, he is just churning around the same stuff. Memories can be deceitful things, for no matter how he thinks he can change the outcome, what he remembers (mostly his guilt over his actions) keeps on tainting the present.

In a film replete with quotable quotes and profound snips of dialog, consider this interchange:

> MAL: You keep telling yourself what you know... but what do you believe? What do you feel?
>
> COBB: Guilt. I feel guilt. And however confused I might get. However lost I might seem...it's always there. Telling me something. Reminding me of the truth.

And, while it did not make *Inception*'s final cut, the script had this provocative back-and-forth between Mal and Cobb:

> MAL: So certain of your world. Of what's real. Do you think *he* is-
>
> ([as she speaks to Adriane and] points at Cobb)

Or do you think he's as lost as I was?

COBB [says defensively]: I know what's real.

MAL: What are the distinguishing characteristics of a dream? Mutable laws of physics? Tell that to the quantum physicists. Reappearance of the dead? What about heaven and hell? Persecution of the dreamer, the creator, the messiah? They crucified Christ, didn't they?

A thought system built on guilt is a philosophy of life in need of repair. Cobb, prompted by Mal, (who is in fact his subconscious speaking out loud, getting the message across by taking on the appearance of his dead wife) is shown here to be taking the first step in healing his mind. To go beyond simple facts that he has rolling around in his brain, Mal confronts him about what he feels.

And his answer is honest! Guilt is his underlying motivation. This guilt follows him (and all of us!) around. It affects everything we do, even if we don't know it. It's woven into the fabric of humanity. Cobb has not learned how to overcome guilt and find peace, but many psycho-spiritual thinkers suggest that it begins by confronting our inner demons.

The lines that didn't make the final cut would have appeared prior to Mal's question "what do you feel?" and Cobb's admission that "I feel guilt." By questioning Cobb's belief system, Mal was helping him recognize that knowledge of "reality" is suspect, but our feelings in the present moment are accessible and true for us. That is, feelings are genuine and unique for each individual. No outside source can *make* us feel our feelings.

Ariadne is pivotal to Cobb's catharsis. It seems likely that Nolan selected her name for its historical import. In Greek mythology Ariadne was the daughter of Minos, King of Crete. He put his daughter in charge of the labyrinth that kept the Minotaur, a half-man and half-bull creature. After a time, she helped a man escape the labyrinth by giving him a spool of string to retrace his steps back to the entrance.

Here we have Cobb hiring Ariadne for her ability to create mazes. Her role in *Inception* provides Cobb with the string to escape the labyrinth of his own guilt. Cobb has struggled for a long time with this guilt, but only with the insightful help of Ariadne does he start to overcome his misery. Throughout *Inception*, Ariadne steps up to offer the more elegant solution to the challenges set before Cobb and the team.

The following line illustrates how Ariadne's insightfulness begins to set Cobb's mind free:

> ARIADNE: Your guilt defines her. Powers her. If we're going to succeed in this, you're going to have to forgive yourself, and you're going to have to confront her. But you don't have to do it alone.

It's been said many times that "All forgiveness is self-forgiveness," but there are times in our lives when this seems an especially important lesson to learn, and we need other people to point the way out when we are lost. Ariadne teaches this lesson to Cobb quite directly, for if he is to be successful in this inception and to ultimately reunite with his children, his debilitating guilt needs to be dealt with...quickly!

As for the last sentence, "But you don't have to do it alone," Ariadne is referring to herself and other friends, but it also seems possible that Nolan was vaguely referencing the notion that we can always ask and receive help from a Higher Power. This "help" may come in different forms, and the timing is often unpredictable or seemingly coincidental.

Let us keep in mind that while Cobb needs to confront Mal, she doesn't actually exist anymore, but is only a figment of his imagination. He really needs to confront himself, for there is no one else!

Cobb has been trying to heal himself by using a more psychoanalytical approach, revisiting his pain in hopes of finding a breakthrough that will release him from his suffering. But Ariadne offers him a *spiritual* solution – look, confront, and then transcend that which has not actually happened. Salvation is not something that can be figured out intellectually, rather, salvation is something that Cobb can allow if he is willing to let go of his guilt.

In some ways, Cobb reinforces his guilt by repeatedly going down that elevator in hopes of finding answers when in actuality he has had the answer all along. Ariadne could be thought of as representing Spirit, where she sees a need and fulfills it by giving guidance where it is needed most. Perhaps paradoxically, Cobb *did* have to go all the way down to release his guilt, but his self-styled elevator was an ineffective means.

As was noted earlier about the Parisian street "projection" scene, Cobb's life continually goes off the rails because he is projecting his subconscious guilt onto his outer world. On the surface, he seems to be high-functioning in his job, but his chaotic inner world jeopardizes his effectiveness. The power of Cobb's mind can make amazing things happen, but contained in all of his accomplishments are also seeds of disaster, seeds that take root and ultimately cancel out his accomplishments.

As many Eastern spiritual philosophies contend, "the call compels the answer." Things happen for a reason, and Adriane comes into Cobb's life at precisely the right time to help him find a way out of his guilt-ridden mind.

Much later in the film, the moment of decision was when Cobb and Ariadne seek to salvage the project by going down into Limbo from the fortified medical facility:

COBB: That's the kick-you have to go!

ARIADNE: You're coming!

COBB: No, I'm not. I'm staying here to find Saito.

(turns to Mal)

And to say goodbye.

Ariadne loosens her grip on the railing...

ARIADNE: Don't lose yourself. Find Saito. And bring him back.

COBB: I will.

...which then bridges to this point:

MAL: We'd be together forever. You promised me.

COBB: I know. But we can't. And I'm sorry.

MAL: You remember when you asked me to marry you? You said you dreamt that we'd grow old together.

COBB: And we did...

Mal looks at Cobb... thinking. Remembering.

INSERT CUT: TWO ELDERLY PEOPLE (MAL AND COBB) WALK THROUGH LIMBO... ACROSS A WASTELAND... TWO ELDERLY HANDS CLUTCH EACH OTHER AS THEY LIE DOWN ON THE RAILROAD TRACK...

COBB: I miss you more than I can bear... but we had our time together. And now I have to let go...

"And now I have to let go." Spiritually speaking, "letting go" is one of the most important notions on many a spiritual path, as well as a difficult mindset to achieve. One truly has to be ready to confront one's guilt with steady nerves and a resolve of steel.

In deconstructing *Inception*, we see that Nolan has artfully exposed Cobb's guilt. He has had the above dialog repeated in some form many times throughout the movie, but without resolution up until this point. He has shown us that it is fruitless to resolve guilt by having Cobb thinking that his memories of Mal could produce an "answer" for his suffering. Instead, his memories were in fact the *source* of his suffering.

Nolan contrasts Cobb's subterranean elevator with the positive and creative "workshop" scene. Here Cobb and the team feel like a highly inventive advertising agency, bouncing ideas around for how to create the most effective inception on Fischer. So now we have a dynamic "outer" world contrasted and covered over with deep hidden secrets.

The question for the team to decide is: what thought do they plant in Fischer's head? Eames suggests an insertion of the thought "'screw you' to the old man," meaning Fischer's father. Revenge seems to be an obvious motive to Eames, and yet Cobb immediately counters: "No. Positive emotion trumps negative emotion every time. We yearn for people to be reconciled, for catharsis. We need positive emotional logic."

Cobb knows the answer is not in the dark thoughts of attack and revenge, but rather in the thoughts that have the positive light of progress. He would rather plant a seed that will work in both the short- and long-term, or are at the very least benign. His term "positive emotional logic" may seem odd to some, for "emotion" and "logic" seem to denote very different ideas. Conventionally, "emotions" are thought of as being divorced from logic. Most think that there is a split between left (analytical) and right (creative) brain functions, and that the two don't meet. Nolan seems to take a different perspective, for this line recognizes that emotions arise from a thought system that transcends a mere sum-of-the-parts approach, one in which the creative and analytical sides of the mind work in tandem.

Actually, emotions arise from triggers that we perceive in time and space (the world), which are then processed by our thought system – our personal philosophy. This set-up is inherent in the human condition. The foundation of all constructs are based on either the thought of "love" or "fear" – emotional states. Hence, "emotional logic" – when looked at this way – makes perfect sense.

And this is the point of this inception project, to replace a key element of Fischer's thought system with a more positive one, one that will stick, one that will motivate Fischer to look at his situation anew.

It's worth noting that Nolan wrote and directed Fischer to be a rather emotionally aloof, controlled character, not a strong personality. His father dominates his life, and young Fischer plays the dutiful, yet quietly resentful, son. This bottled-up, introspective young man may be more prone to having an inception performed successfully on him.

On the other hand (and maybe even because of this), young Fischer has been professionally trained against such an onslaught, his subconscious has been "militarized," that is, he now has extremely strong defense mechanisms. This makes performing an inception on him extremely difficult. The idea that Fischer hired a firm that trained him to protect *his thoughts* is a severe one. That's how "advanced" society has become in *Inception*, where not only is material wealth, or digital computer secrets, protected by a vast array of security measures, our private thoughts are also in need of protection.

It is a challenging prospect to find the "right" idea to insert, especially as that seed idea will have to slowly spool out over time in the proper direction. For the idea to *really* "take," it has to sit well with young Robert. An idea that is planted is far more likely to be rejected if it doesn't make sense to him on a lot of levels.

They know that the "seed" was successful based on Fisher's emotional reaction when he opens the safe and discovers the hand-made pinwheel that was presumably put there by the team. Symbolically, Fischer rediscovers his innocence, releasing a lifetime of guilt and fears with a good cry when he realizes that he'd been mistaken all along. The elder Fischer tells him in the hospital complex's strong-room that "I was disappointed...*that you tried*," Fischer's emotional/logical thought system is opened up.

Later, when Fischer and Browning (who is really Eames disguised as Browning, and is known in *Inception* as "The Forger") make it to shore from the now-submerged van, Robert reinterprets his father's "alternative" will, which he marveled at in the dreamscape's strong-room. "The will means that Dad wanted me to be my own man, not live for him," Fischer tells Browning.

This "incepted" idea was successful and has taken firm root in Fischer's mind. *Inception*'s denouement implies that Fischer would follow through on this idea of Robert being his "own man," which we're led to believe involves him breaking up Fischer Morrow Corporation, the family dynasty.

The 747

Consider the climactic scene near the end of *Inception*, where the team (plus Fischer) awaken in the 747 from their path-breaking caper. After having gone three dreams down – with Saito, Ariadne, Fischer, and Cobb going down to Limbo as well – they awaken in the airliner with a profound sense of satisfaction, having accomplished something unprecedented.

Nolan's allegory works on a more profound metaphysical level. In fact, *nothing has happened* – not really. Six people have taken a long flight during which they were sedated and unconscious. Everything that "happened" happened only in their dreams, a *shared* dream but a dream nevertheless.

There is no dialog in this scene to speak of, for there is nothing really *to* say. And, yet, the looks on the main character's faces speak volumes. They have shared the holiest of experiences, a transcendent sense screams off the screen at the viewer.

Here is the relevant passage of the shooting script that Nolan directs so masterfully:

INT. FIRST CLASS CABIN, 747 - DAY

    Ariadne watches Cobb. His eyes are closed.

FLIGHT ATTENDANT (O.S.): Hot towel, sir?

    His EYES FLICKER OPEN. He takes the towel with a nod. Ariadne smiles. Relieved.

FLIGHT ATTENDANT: We'll be landing in Los Angeles in about twenty minutes. Do you need immigration forms?

    Cobb nods. Takes a landing card. Looks around the cabin.

    Saito is WATCHING him. Serious. Haunted. Holding Cobb's gaze, SAITO PICKS UP THE PHONE AND DIALS. Cobb nods thanks...

That's all it says. And yet the camera rolls for one minute that feels like 15, slowly scanning the team. The music swells subtly yet overwhelmingly. The looks on each player's face is unmistakable, part war heroes returning from the front, part angels experiencing the most sublime of epiphanies.

As the sequencing in *Inception* can be hard to track, a very careful following of the storyline reveals that it is coherent. This final 747 scene is setup by the rapid intercut scenes from a few minutes earlier. Recall how a few crescendos were happening at once. While the van hit the water, Arthur was blasting the elevator, and the fortified medical facility was exploding.

Intercut among all the scenes of destruction, the players in the film are all waking up. All, that is, except Cobb.

Cobb has come to the point where he can handle facing his guilt, he now can let Mal go. As he said in the penthouse apartment in Limbo when Cobb says "... but we had our time together. And now I have to let go...."

Cobb's Resurrection

As the team begins to regroup at the van level – one down from the 747 – Arthur expresses concern for Cobb to Ariadne, as they swim to shore having escaped from the van. Cobb is still there – in the water, unconscious. Arthur says to her, "He'll be lost...." But with a quiet certainty, Ariadne comes back, "No. He'll be all right."

Ariadne simply knows that Cobb has more work to do.

After letting Mal go, Cobb needs to find Saito. When he's brought to see Saito, the dialog is rich, despite its brevity:

SAITO: So... have you come to kill me?

Cobb does not look up.

SAITO: I've been waiting for someone to come for me...

COBB: Someone from your half-remembered dream...?

Saito peers at Cobb.

SAITO: Cobb? Not possible – he and I were young men together. And I am an old man...

COBB: Filled with regret?

Saito REMEMBERS, nods...

SAITO: Waiting to die alone, yes.

Cobb is STARING at something on the table.

COBB: I came back for you... I came to remind you of what you once knew...

> Cobb gestures at the table. Saito follows his gaze down to the polished surface of the table...

COBB: That this world is not real.

Spiritual philosophies such as some forms of Hinduism, Buddhism, and ACIM posit the notion that the material world is illusory, or not real. The Sanskrit term for this is "Maya," which Wikipedia notes is "usually quoted as 'illusion,' centered on the fact that we do not experience the environment itself but rather a projection of it, created by us."[6]

The scene in *Inception* continues with Cobb giving the top a spin:

> The top IS STILL SPINNING PERFECTLY, AS IF IT WILL NEVER TOPPLE. Saito looks at the top. Then back to Cobb.

SAITO: You came to convince me to honor our arrangement?

COBB: Yes. And to take a leap of faith.

The script suggests this *quid pro quo*. And, yet, in the film itself, Cobb actually says, "To take a leap of faith, yes."

This language used in the final cut of *Inception* is far more ambiguous. Cobb is less invested in the outcome. The written script's words are all about getting something in exchange from Saito; the film's actual dialog suggests that Cobb has no expectations about what Saito will do, just that he urges Saito to take this leap of faith.

Nolan is a careful, methodical screenwriter, it is notable that the term "leap of faith" is used three times in *Inception*. These instances include:

- In the helicopter when Saito first proposes hiring Cobb to perform an inception.

- Before Mal leaps to her death from the hotel, she suggests that Cobb take a leap of faith.

- And now Cobb suggesting that Saito take a leap of faith.

There are also four (or five, depending on how one counts them) safes in *Inception*. They are:

- The safe in Saito's elegant dining room. Note that Cobb says during this scene to a young Saito: "If this is a dream and you have a safe full of secrets, I need to know what's in that safe."

- The safe in the young girl's bedroom that Ariadne stumbles on when she follows Cobb down the elevator of his subconscious.

- Inside a doll house in Mal's childhood home in Limbo there is a safe that contains a top.

- And, of course, the safe in the strong room in the hospital complex on the "snow level." That's the safe next to the elder Fischer's bed, the one containing both his will and the pinwheel. In a sense, this strong room is itself a safe, making the safe next to the elder Fischer's bed a safe within a safe.

"Safes," "safety" and other forms of defense are critical to understanding *Inception*. Safes, of course, are a rich metaphor for the subconscious tendency to "squirrel away" our most personal thoughts and memories, as well as our deepest fears – all of the things we cannot face, as of yet. Safes and safety are rich themes from a psycho-spiritual perspective. If we are emotional beings, driven by love or fear, then for us to experience the positive "allness" of love, our job becomes to undo fear (or, technically, to ask a Higher Power to help us undo it) in our consciousness. As Cobb says during the scene when the team is planning the Fischer inception:

> COBB: Now, the subconscious motivates through emotion, not reason, so we have to translate the idea into an emotional concept.

However, defensiveness – represented by the safes in *Inception* – is where we hide our innocence away from the cruel, brutal world that we perceive.

Very early in the film, when Cobb meets with a Young Saito in an architected dream level, Cobb and Arthur, as salesmen are wont to do, are pitching Saito. Their objective is to teach him to protect his mind from "extractions." These are similar in nature to "inceptions," except that in an extraction, thoughts are stolen, not planted. At one point during this pitch, Cobb tells Saito, "You need to *completely* let me in."

What is interesting about this is: In a sense, it is true, although not as Cobb means it here. Instead, many psycho-spiritual thinkers assert that we need to let truth completely into our minds. Self-deception of any kind is unacceptable. There can be no secrets if one's mind is to be truly free and, as it is purified, it needs no defense. Defenses, in this sense, create the need for defenses. As ACIM states: "In my defenselessness my safety lies."[5] Only with complete self-honesty can we make ourselves invulnerable to the "slings and arrows of outrageous fortune," as Shakespeare has put it.

Even so, Cobb is not being completely honest with Saito; Cobb has a hidden agenda. Cobb and his team architected this Japanese castle to extract secrets from Saito, secrets that are also held in a safe.

Even more pregnantly, since Cobb himself is conflicted (guilt-ridden by his memories of Mal), the whole setup begins to fall apart. Then, much to the chagrin of the whole team, Mal enters, proclaiming, in effect, that the jig is up.

Mal teaches us an important lesson about the inner workings of the dreamscape. She has a gun, and we learn that the dream will end if she kills Arthur. Normally, if we are killed in a dream, we wake up from it. However, Mal notes, "Killing him would just wake him up...but pain? Pain is in the mind...."

A profoundly important insight, this one! When Mal shoots Arthur in the leg, we assume that is where the pain is. However, since the body is not in fact shot, how could it feel anything? In the dreamscape (and, for that matter, in reality), Arthur's leg is hurt, yes, but the pain that he feels from that wound is in his mind, for there is where sensory data is interpreted and labeled "pain."

Cobb quickly kills Arthur in the dream, releasing him from his pained state. One dream level up, the puppet masters of this scene are assembled – *sans* Mal – and they recognize that the architected Japanese castle caper has failed. The story switches back and forth, as an earthquake begins to destroy the castle. Amid the chaos, Cobb realizes that the information in Saito's safe is worthless.

At that point in the movie, everything unravels. The castle falls apart on one level of the dream and rioters burst into the apartment on another.

Limbo, the deepest dream level, is also ever-crumbling whenever we see it. It is a hodge-podge of memories as well, as we find when Cobb and Ariadne walk about the city that Mal and Cobb had built together. Recall, for example, when Cobb and Ariadne were walking through this city, and we see the couple's first house as well as the house that Mal grew up in. Her childhood home was sandwiched into a dense urban jungle, complete with a moat that our eye recognizes as anomalous in a cityscape.

How do we "know" what we know? Mal pokes this age-old notion with the only sensible answer: we don't! She tells him: "You keep telling yourself what you know…but what do you believe? What do you feel?"

In other words, Cobb believes he "knows" things (e.g. facts, observations) but, like most of us, he takes what he knows for granted. Instead, it's more honest to say that we *believe* in the things we *think* we know. Nolan is giving us a lesson in epistemology, reminding us that we don't actually know what we know, only because we don't actually possess knowledge, we only *think* we do! If life is "but a dream," we only operate our lives based on memories of past experiences, which are distorted, selective, and subject to limited, imperfect perceptions. And the honest truth is that Cobb believes he is guilty, and that belief pervades his experience, whether he is conscious of it in any given moment, or not.

So, as the three levels of dreams explode, and start folding back in on themselves, Cobb holds Mal in his arms one last time. She dies to him there both figuratively and literally because he has resolved his guilt. He then carries on with his mission to save Saito and goes deeper into Limbo. As Cobb washes up on the shore of what we now know as Limbo, it is the exact same scene that was enacted earlier in the film, except that the two children are not seen playing in the sand. This is significant, since they were memories of Cobb's children that had been haunting him (showing up in different dreamscapes) throughout the film. By them not being there this time shows us again that he has resolved his subconscious guilt over leaving them motherless.

As he's brought to the dining room of the castle and seated with a 90-year-old Saito, we can't help but notice that something has changed – rather dramatically – about Cobb.

This elderly Saito, having lost himself for a very long time in Limbo, is confused that Cobb appears to be a young man while he is a very old one. Saito had not only thoroughly forgotten his true identity, but was also struggling to remember a long-forgotten but familiar face. Cobb, newly arrived in Limbo, the place of forgetfulness, was also in danger of forgetting his *own* identity, but their back-and-forth dialog stimulated each other's memory.

Time has rushed ahead for Saito, but Cobb has in a sense turned back the hands of time. He has regained his own innocence, having let Mal go. Retrieving Saito amounts to the final piece of the puzzle of resolving Cobb's deep-seated inner turmoil. Ultimately, as they both remember who they are, the elderly Saito nods in agreement to go back with Cobb to the real world.

There's No Place like Home

Like the trailblazing spiritual masterpiece *The Wizard of Oz, Inception* is all about Cobb's desire to "go home." The first instance we see of this burning aspiration of his was during the failed extraction of Saito from a hotel room in Japan. We see Cobb talking to his children on the phone, and his son James says: "When are you coming home?"

Also, during the helicopter scene, Saito induces Cobb by saying: "How would you like to go home? To America. To your children."

Later Arthur says to Cobb when they are in a private jet: "I know how much you want to go home," to which Cobb responds sharply, "No, you don't."

And last but not least, as Ariadne is walking Cobb through her dream architectural models, he says: "I need to get home. That's all I care about right now." He is single-minded, focused, determined.

Indeed, Cobb's determination raises one of the great ethical questions in *Inception*. Recall that the way to wake from a dream is to be killed, according to the world that Nolan has invented. However, Yusuf (played by Dileep Rao) – "The Chemist" – has added a twist to the plot by creating a very powerful sedative.

The team learns in the warehouse on the "van level," much to their dismay, that the sedative is *so* powerful that death in a dream no longer releases a person from the dream. This is revealed by Cobb after Saito has been shot by Fischer's militarized subconscious. Instead of waking up from the dream by being "killed," they would be plunged into Limbo, which Arthur describes as "raw, infinite subconscious," and where all is lost and forgotten.

All the team members, save Cobb and Yusuf, had signed up for this assignment with the expectation that the ultimate escape valve from a dream was death. Now, however, because of Yusuf's high-potency formula, escape-by-death is no longer an option. When the team confronts Cobb about this sin of omission on his part, he responds that "I did what I had to do to get back to my children." We as viewers understand Cobb's motive, but it seems unjustified to allow the team to proceed based on a blatantly false premise.

Cobb seems unapologetic about his deception. But, he concludes in one of the most pregnant lines in *Inception*, "Downwards is the only way forwards. We have to carry on." Spiritually speaking, the most effective means to address suffering is to transcend it by diving deeply into it, to confront it directly.

And this – in a nutshell – is what *Inception* is all about. Cobb's team certainly dives deep, an unprecedented three levels down, to undo and remake Fischer's thought system. And, along the way, Cobb experiences a catharsis regarding his personal demon, his guilt about Mal's suicide.

Totems, *"Non, Je Ne Regrette Rien,"* Kicks, and Trains

Nolan uses repetition – without being repetitive! – throughout *Inception* as a means to keep this complex project on an even keel for the viewer. He introduces a totem on the first page of the screenplay, Cobb's spinning top. As Arthur explains to Ariadne, the purpose of the totem is so that "[y]ou know, beyond a doubt, that you're not in someone else's dream."

A totem grounds a person who explores dreamscapes. While it can become easy to lose oneself, to forget what is a dream and what is reality, the totem is the consistent reminder for members of the *Inception* team. In a sense, totems also have deep spiritual significance. It could represent, for instance, the memory of God/Heaven that each of us has, *when we are conscious enough to remember to remember.*

Finally, the totem is something that is personal, individualized. Each player in *Inception* chooses his or her own totem, imbuing it with special symbolic meaning. This is an interesting contrast with organized religion, which for the most part has a specific set of ritualized symbols that are to be used by all followers.

Another significant repetitive thread in *Inception* is the song by Edith Piaf, *"Non, Je Ne Regrette Rien."* The English translation is: "No, I regret nothing." This song is played to trigger the team when their time is up in the dreamscape. (An interesting aside, Marion Cotillard – Mal in *Inception* – portrayed Edith Piaf in the film "La Vie En Rose.")

As a master filmmaker, Nolan uses this song to subtly say that a life of regrets is a sad and lonely way to live. Nolan prominently offers an illustration of Cobb and Saito's shared concern about becoming old men, "filled with regret, waiting to die alone." Yes, it would be much better to live a full life without regret, forgiving oneself for any supposed transgression, because it is, after all, only a dream. Being guilt-free, having no regrets, is a deeply spiritually significant idea. Waking up to the truth of one's fundamental innocence is the point of the spiritual path.

And then there's "the kick." As Cobb explains, the kick is, "That feeling of falling which snaps you awake. We use that to jolt ourselves awake once we're done." Spiritually speaking, the kick is a "miracle." It's an inflection point, the time that the lesson is completed, and it's time to move on.

Because the team's inception plot is so complex, involving three levels of dreams, all designed to set Fischer up for a major change of mind, the "miracle" will need to be especially potent. Unlike the miracles that Jesus is reported to have performed, these "kicks" in *Inception* are more like the way the word "miracle" is used in ACIM, which defines the word as a "shift in perception from fear to love."[6]

As Cobb says: "The trick is to devise a kick for each level, then synchronize them to get a snap that penetrates all three layers." The plan is that the team needs to be reminded of the ancient melody of "no regrets," delivered in the form of *"Non, Je Ne Regrette Rien."* This reminder is then followed by major trajectory-altering, miraculous kicks to wake the team back into reality. An outrageously bold plan, this. As it turns out, the plan works like a charm, albeit with some improvisations.

Throughout *Inception*, we see Cobb's dreams turned to nightmares of misfortune, often represented by a train. Why did Nolan choose trains to serve in this symbolic purpose? Certainly we know that it was used as a kick to get Cobb and Mal back from Limbo. But since it was the means of bringing them back to reality that ended in Mal's suicide, it also becomes representative of the source of guilt in Cobb's mind. He therefore subconsciously uses it to wreak disaster in his dreamscapes.

Here are some examples of trains making an impact:

- The team's first-level dream turns from the smoothly functioning carjacking of Fischer to a train barreling through city streets, putting a kink in the caper.

- In the opening sequence of Inception, after the extraction from Saito fails, we see Cobb and Arthur on a bullet train in Japan. Nolan foreshadows Cobb's problem with trains as he tells Arthur, "I can't stand trains."

- When Cobb is testing Yusuf's sedative by going under himself, he has a brief dream in which Mal's head lies on a train track as a train barrels toward her.

- When Ariadne and Mal first meet during the Ariadne-down-the-elevator sequence, this pregnant back-and-forth involving trains unfolds:

  Mal moves slowly towards Ariadne...

  MAL: I'll tell you a riddle. You're waiting for a train. A train that will take you far away. You know where you hope this train will take you, but you don't know for sure...

  Mal glides around Ariadne, looking her over.

  MAL: But... it *doesn't matter*. How can it not matter to you where that train will take you?

COBB (O.S. [off screen]): Because you'll be together.

This is a deeply spiritual concept, subtly put. It puts in perspective that worldly outcomes do not matter, what *does* matter is "who" one does it with. Although Cobb is obviously talking about the person one does an activity with, from a spiritual perspective, one could take this to mean that what matters is whether one is in the world with spirit or ego. If one is "in spirit," all is love and all is well. If one is "in ego," all is fear and all is not well.

In the present moment, then, all is binary: either all love or all fear. (This is a theme in *The Matrix* as well, which used the binary nature of computer code to set the stage for that film.) However, because the mind has been trained to tell itself figurative stories over time, the mind tends to flit back and forth at light speed between love and fear. These fugues of emotional states have different names; periods dominated by love thoughts might be labeled "happiness," while fear-dominated stretches might be "sad" ones. In other words, there are many different labels for the only two core, emotional states.

Viral Ideas

Inception illustrates the power of the idea and the primacy of consciousness. The physical universe may seem to be the repository of magnificence, but if the magnificence is unperceived by consciousness, it is for all intents and purposes without existence. The tree may well fall in the forest, but without a conscious mind to hear and discern the tree falling, nothing – in a sense – has happened. In other words, in a universe with no life and no consciousness, the sound of a tree falling in the forest would not be heard or labeled as a "sound." Hearing a sound requires consciousness to hear it!

As Cobb explains to Saito early in *Inception*:

COBB: You see, an idea is like a virus...Resilient...Highly contagious, and an idea can grow. The smallest seed of an idea can grow to define or destroy your world...

Certainly we have seen the disastrous results of this idea in Cobb's architectural designs. Even so, those who view the material world as being the only thing that is real may have a hard time with Cobb's assertion, particularly the ability of an idea to "define" or "destroy" one's world. This statement implies that the world is subject to change by thoughts and that it is defined by perceptions.

Ideas – or, more properly, consciousness – are eternal. The material world is temporary, meaning that things "too shall pass." The eternal will not, being eternal. Throughout *Inception*, ideas and dreams are shared with the aid of a shared-dreaming mechanism that employs Yusuf's special sedative.

The shared-dream idea seems to be nod to Carl Jung and his theory of a collective unconscious. Cobb and his team share these dreams to the point where the dream becomes their reality.

In a television interview with Canadian movie website www.tribute.ca, Nolan summed up his intentions with *Inception* by saying: "I really want people to be entertained and invigorated...and then hopefully they'll find certain things or ideas about it afterwards that might rattle around their brains...."[7]

In a way, Nolan is performing *an inception* on the viewer, planting ideas in our heads while entertaining us at the same time!

Planting idea seeds while entertaining seems benign enough. But this doesn't begin to address what Nolan was really doing with *Inception*, since humans are – at root – idea machines. We cannot avoid having ideas, since consciousness is, after all, what defines us. We could use Nolan's exercise to challenge dysfunctional ideas and replace them with helpful ones.

And even *that* doesn't quite nail it. Much of *Inception* is about uncovering hidden ideas first, examining them, tossing out the harmful ones and then replacing them with helpful ones. For example, both Fischer's and Cobb's fundamental thoughts are in safes. Much of this film involves removing these hidden ideas and examining them for purposes of personal liberation.

Consider the picture of young Fischer and his dad, which is shown a few times in the film. Presenting this picture this way suggests that much of the human condition involves burying the germ of an idea, be it negative or positive. A story is told about the idea, and a lifetime of emotions and/or guilt is created around it. On some level, this buried idea is always known to us; this implies that we *know* the source of our discontent...and it takes a tremendous amount of effort for us to remain in denial of it. But deny it we do, until we are ready to face it.

When Fischer regains his pinwheel, the slate is cleaned and he regains his innocence, which of course he never really lost. It was there all the time. Much like Dorothy in the *Wizard of Oz*, who longed for Home, but had never left!

Despite the fact that Fischer is considered the "mark" in *Inception*, it's also the case that he benefits greatly from the entire process, even though it is an arduous road. First kidnapped; then later manipulated by being made aware that he is dreaming by Cobb playing "Rod Green, marketing"; to later becoming an active, gun-toting participant in the inception. We could view Fischer as suffering from the Stockholm Syndrome, akin to a male Patty Hearst, the heiress who was kidnapped by a terrorist organization only to later join the terrorists and participate in a bank robbery.

In a sense, *Inception* illustrates the saying: "God helps those who help themselves," as we see Fischer grow from a timid, aloof young man living in his father's shadow into a far more assertive, decisive figure.

Fischer believes that his father found it disappointing that the son was not like his elder, but the son's core ideas are changed to believe that Maurice Fischer was disappointed that his boy even *tried* to emulate him. Cobb's team had endeavored successfully to replace the childhood-disappointment theme in Fischer's life with a new idea, one designed to change his final behavior. This revelation comes just before Robert opens the safe to discover his long-lost, hand-made pinwheel, representing his innocence. Yes, young Fischer will break his company up due to Cobb's team's manipulation, but we get the sense that he is also liberated in the process because he recaptures his belief in himself.

As for *Inception*'s conclusion, many have asked the question: Does the top ever stop spinning? As Cobb leaves the frame to be with his beloved children, the camera angles on and then dollies closer to the top as it spins on the dining-room table. We detect a wobble, but the frame cuts to black, leaving us guessing: Does it topple, or not? Is Cobb back in the real world, or is this world a dream, too?

On one level, Nolan wants to leave the theater guessing: does the top fall, or not? On another level, the writer/director may be suggesting an entirely different angle. We notice that Cobb is unconcerned about whether the top topples or not. He walks away. The joy he feels in being reunited with this children is all that matters to him. If this too is a dream, so be it! If it's a dream, it's a happy one, and that is what counts for Cobb.

We all may be living in a Grand Illusion, in Maya. While here, we create our own meaning, our own emotional states, our own loves and likes and preferences. While living in this dreamstate, it is 100% on us as individuals to make our own joy.

One has the distinct sense that Christopher Nolan is making his own joy by making this masterpiece known simply as *Inception*. Whether this life is all one big dream or quite real matters not. Nolan and the team that made *Inception* have produced a film that delights and provokes thought in a breathtaking, provocative manner.

Endnotes for *Inception*

1. Some have suggested that there is a fourth dreamscape, called the "building level." This is where buildings are perpetually crumbling. Others suggest that this building level and the place where Cobb washes up on shore and then meets old Saito are two different parts of Limbo. For our purposes in this book, these are technicalities that distract from this deconstruction.
For more discussion on this technicality, see:
Eternality Tan, "Is 'Building Level' Limbo?" @Filmnomenon, (2010), filmiliarnews.blogspot.com/2010/09/is-building-level-limbo.html

2. FAQ for Inception (2010), www.imdb.com/title/tt1375666/faq

3. *A Course in Miracles*, (Glen Ellen, CA: Foundation for Inner Peace, 1992) T-27.VII.13:1-2

4. Kenneth Wapnick, Ph.D., "The Happy Dream," Foundation for A Course in Miracles, www.facim.org/online-learning-aids/excerpt-series/ the-happy-dream/part-viii.aspx

5. *A Course in Miracles*, (Glen Ellen, CA: Foundation for Inner Peace, 1992) W-153

6. "An Introduction," Foundation for A Course in Miracles, acim.org/AboutACIM/

7. Video interview by Bonnie Laufer of Christopher Nolan on www.tribute.ca, http://www.tribute.ca/interviews/ christopher-nolan-inception/director/19428/

Revolver: Your mind will not accept a game this big

Revolver is a film that is easily misunderstood, to the extent it can *be* understood. It had a checkered past of being released and then re-released, in part because it is such a deceivingly complex film – having more layers than an onion – that mainstream reviewers generally dismissed it as a not-very-well done gangster movie from the popular filmmaker Guy Ritchie. The British writer/director was known for more linear, comprehensible gangster films (*Snatch, Lock, Stock and Two Smoking Barrels*). As Ritchie married Madonna in 2000 and proceeded to remake *Swept Away* – which bombed – *Revolver* was promoted as Ritchie returning to his gangster-genre roots.

Instead, it became pretty clear to the viewer that this effort was not "just" a gangster movie. It was speculated that Ritchie's script was heavily influenced by Kabbalah (Jewish mysticism), which he and Madonna both practice. Mainstream reviewers implied that *Revolver* was a confusing bait-and-switch attempt: Make it look like a gangster movie while proselytizing his religious views.

Ritchie summarily denies that *Revolver* has anything to do with his religious beliefs. He said: "There aren't any Kabbalah references. At one stage somebody called it a Kabbalah script, which was a mystery to me."[1]

Still, we can say that this film is certainly not simply another run-of-the-mill gangster movie. In the tradition of *Fight Club* and *Mulholland Drive*, *Revolver* is a film that can be viewed through multiple lenses. It is one of the rare films that can (and should!) be watched numerous times. Each viewing reveals a new aspect, a different nuance. Because it's a non-linear film as is *Mulholland Drive*, (meaning it goes back and forth between past, present, and future, not just a story told in a straight-line sequence from start to finish) it seems nearly impossible to "get" *Revolver* in just one viewing. Possibly with the help of this deconstruction the viewer will have an easier time of deciphering the inner workings of this subtly remarkable film.

Breaking down and understanding what *Revolver* is all about is no easy task, and it has no one "correct" interpretation. It's as if Guy Ritchie has given us a film that is wide-open to an individualized interpretation; you are free to make what you want of the film. This book's deconstruction provides you with one such take on this profound movie. It seems helpful to dive into *Revolver* by observing the main characters.

Jake Green

Jake Green (played by Jason Statham) is the protagonist, the man whose arc we invest in. His is a titanic journey, the only journey, the journey of self-discovery that each of us is on, whether we realize it or not.

Revolver could be viewed as a "jailbreak" film, as Ritchie himself told an interviewer:

> "The film starts off with a jailbreak and ends with a jailbreak because all the skullduggery going on inside his head didn't allow him to know he was still incarcerated. That's what the film is about, the ultimate jailbreak and the radical actions one needs to undertake to liberate oneself from this jail. It tells the story of the skullduggery and trickery and head-trickery that accompanies Jake on his journey, and the seemingly unlikely actions our hero has to undertake to break out of his jail."[2]

Technically, Ritchie is not quite accurate in his comments here. In the opening scene, Jake is *released from* prison, it's *not* a "jailbreak," per se, as Ritchie's quote says. Later Jake recounts that while in prison – solitary confinement! – his cell was situated between a conman and a chess master. During this seven-year stint, much is shared among these three. They spend the time passing chess moves among the cells. They read up on advanced scientific theory. And they scheme about one day escaping the confines of this prison together. It's important to note that the three convicts never once meet each other face to face.

One day, Jake finds that the conman and the chess master have unexpectedly vanished; it's as if they were never there. They leave no signs of how they escaped, or where they went. Jake, however, realizes that he was conned, they never had any intention of taking him with them. Not only did they *not* take him, but Jake later learns that they have taken all of his booty that was hidden on the outside from previous crimes.

Despite this injustice, eventually Jake does get out of prison and he uses the knowledge he gleaned from the conman and the chess master to amass a great fortune of his own within two years as a professional gambler.

Billy Green, Jake's brother, tells Jake, "You've got more money than you could ever spend." What Ritchie may be pointing to here is that Jake "Green" – the color of money – has been consumed with amassing green paper strips without any real purpose. Jake seems loyal to his family and friends, but he also seems very much the lone wolf. He has no romantic relationships or friendships other than his brother. He's all about money at this point.

The name "Green" also suggests "newness." This also tracks with the Jake Green character, as he ultimately experiences an epiphany, a reinvention (or recognition) of who he is within. His outward appearance remains the same, but *Revolver* in the end is a film about undoing the fear that defines each and every one of us. On the outside we may look the same as we always did, but the inner transformation has completely changed what we are all about.

Jake Green is a similar figure to Mr. Anderson, a.k.a., Neo, the character Keanu Reeves plays in *The Matrix*. *Revolver* is in this sense yet another take on the Plato's Cave parable, as the lone person who sees that reality is not what they thought it was. *(See Appendix A for more on Plato's Cave.)*

Whereas Mr. Anderson becomes Neo through a process of choosing the red pill over the blue, and then unplugging from the Matrix – a taxing, physically painful process – Jake Green's awakening process is less science fiction and more of an internal non-fiction, but painful nevertheless. These metaphysical movies outline the arduous process of the chrysalis struggling to transform into a butterfly, and its success is heralded by becoming a new creature.

Throughout most of *Revolver*, we are offered Jake's inner thoughts through the skillful use of voice-overs. At times Jake's inner voice(s) seem to be contradictory, as if he is alternatively listening to two voices that offer very different perspectives.

The story edges forward when Jake approaches Dorothy Macha (played by Ray Liotta), his former employer for whom Jake had taken the fall and gone to prison. (As we'll take up later, the only other character whose inner thoughts we can hear is Macha's. And, yes, Liotta's character's name is "Dorothy," a point also to be taken up later. Macha's employees call him "Mr. D.")

In part, Jake's following actions are motivated by revenge. He says of Macha, "I need to see him squirm." His goal is to be set up in a business like Macha, who owns a casino and other apparently criminal enterprises. Even though Jake has a deep-seated phobia about elevators, he takes one up to see Macha. He doesn't like the feeling of being trapped, which is understandable for a person who'd been in solitary confinement for seven years. As he rides the elevator, he says to himself, "Why should a man do what he doesn't like to do?" This is key to understanding Jake, both in terms of *Revolver*'s narrative and on psycho-spiritual and metaphysical level. "Prison" and "fear of tight spaces" recur for Jake, not only physically, but in his mind.

The Jake/Macha meeting is contentious, where Macha scoffs at Jake's desire to be set up in business. "You're a man who needs a master," Macha derisively tells Jake. "You're an employee." Jake turns the tables on him by betting and winning a very large amount of money from Macha's casino.

It gets worse. Macha decides that Jake is too much of a threat and decides to put a hit out on him.

On exiting the casino, a man we later learn is named Zach (played by Vincent Pastore, from *The Sopranos*) approaches Jake and says, "You're in trouble, Mr. Green. We can help." Zach hands Jake a card, which Jake reads quickly and then strides off. He looks at the elevator, but opts to take the stairs. At the top of the stairs, Jake collapses, tumbling to the bottom. The camera reveals that the card Zach handed Jake says, "Take the elevator."

This plants the seed that Zach possesses some sort of magical abilities. In this sense, we see that Jake's inability to face his fear of tight spaces leads to him hurting himself, badly. Disregarding Zach's prescient counsel has proven to be a big mistake.

After being released from the hospital, Jake – along with some colleagues – head home. As he begins to unlock the door, he sees another card at his feet, a card similar to the one Zach gave him earlier. It says: "Pick this up." This time, Jake obeys, which is a good thing since at that moment, shots ring out and those who are with Jake are killed. Suddenly, in the midst of this carnage, Zach pulls up in a car, fends off Macha's hit men, and rescues Jake.

Jake is learning that it may be in his best interest to trust Zach, albeit with reservations. Zach takes him to a club named PARAMOUNT CITY. This is a clue from Ritchie that something important is about to happen. The word "paramount" means "of supreme importance." We see that Paramount City is a pool hall in the front room, a chess club in the back.

Billiards is a physical, kinetic game. Chess is entirely cerebral. Jake and Zach pass through the pool hall, making their way into the chess parlor. Symbolically, they are crossing over from the material world of bodies and money to a spiritual realm of emotion and mind.

Zach introduces Jake to Avi (played by Andre Benjamin). Avi is black, and it becomes clear that Zach – who is white – and Avi are a team. Interestingly, on the flip side of the coin, Macha is white, and his lieutenant is black, a man named French Paul (played by Terence Maynard).

It may be that Ritchie was purposely setting up two yin/yang pairings, with Avi/Zach being the path of liberation for Jake, with the Macha/Paul pairing representing wrong-minded materialism. Note, too, that Avi and Zach's initials are A and Z, or the beginning and the end. This clue from Ritchie will become more significant later in this deconstruction.

Avi has somehow obtained Jake's medical records from his hospital stay, telling him, "You will die within three days." Jake distrusts this, but doesn't totally dismiss it either, since they've been right so far. These unlikely guardian angels claim they can save Jake, but it will come at a cost. Avi and Zach tell him that they will bleed him dry, and take all of his newly earned money. In addition, Jake is to "do as we tell you, without argument." Then, and only then, will they give him the means to be saved.

While Avi and Zach lay down their conditions, Jake's voice-over "ego chatter" becomes especially contrary. Jake tells himself that he's being conned, but Zach immediately volunteers that "it's only natural that you think that you are somehow being conned, but think a little harder."

Ritchie is subtly establishing here that Zach and Avi can read Jake's mind. Despite this seeming "magic" that they've already performed, Jake is so resistant to what they are saying that he misses this miracle, and is incapable of "thinking a little harder." The fact that they took all of his money and made him subservient to them challenges Jake to such a high degree that his ego defense mechanisms are on high alert.

In one of the most pregnant – yet easily missed – lines in the film, Avi tells Jake, "You don't have a lot of time, and in reality you don't have a choice." Despite appearances, Avi and Zach are serving as the Holy Spirit (the terms "Higher Self" or "conscience" could describe their function in *Revolver* as well) for Jake. Their purpose becomes teaching Jake lessons in humility and forgiveness, educating him about which voice in his head he should listen to. Avi's statement tips his hand when he comments that there is no choice, suggesting a fatalistic perspective.

According to the Stanford Encyclopedia of Philosophy, "Though the word 'fatalism' is commonly used to refer to an attitude of resignation in the face of some future event or events which are thought to be inevitable, philosophers usually use the word to refer to the view that we are powerless to do anything other than what we actually do."[3]

As Ritchie himself said in an interview:

> "I don't believe chance exists, no. I don't know whether it does but personally I don't believe in it. Either there's order in the universe or there's chaos. Either everything is predetermined or, by the definition of free choice, you can determine it but there's still no element of chance. Or there's the other way of thinking, that it's all chaos and there's absolutely no order and it's all chance. You either subscribe to one or the other. I subscribe to the idea that there is order although it may look like total chaos, but I've no idea if I'm right."[4]

Hardcore non-dualists take "fate" or predetermination in a different direction. Time and space are not real – they're illusory. What appears to be a "choice" is choiceless, not because it was "meant to be," but because what appear to be "choices" are actually just false images. As Ramana Maharshi, one of the foremost non-dualist teachers, put it: "It is like a cinema. The screen is always there but several types of pictures appear on the screen and then disappear. Nothing sticks to the screen, it remains a screen."[5]

In other words, the appearance of a "choice" is just lights flickering on a screen, it is not really a choice at all, there just *appears* to be one.

So, for Jake there really is no choice, even though it *appears* that he has one. He did seem to make a choice to not heed the warning to take the elevator, but that didn't work out so well for him. He made a choice to pick up the second card, and thus avoided being shot. Chaos or predetermination are not quite the right terms; the lessons that unfold before us do seem to be either randomly generated or part of a divinely guided plan.

If we are honest, we really don't know what the cause is of any effect or outcome, or even if the "effect" or choice is the "right" one for us at the moment. Yet, in life, as we are confronted with choices, we do attempt to pick the one that seems to be in our best interest. Many spiritual teachers have wisely counseled against investing emotionally in the outcomes of our choices; instead, they suggest to simply do our best and choose the kinder, more loving option. Whatever the outcome of our choices ends up being, it seems healthier to perceive that choice as the correct one. Second-guessing our decisions would always lead away from serenity.

As singer/songwriter Alanis Morissette put it so beautifully in her song *Utopia*:

> We would share and listen and support and welcome
> Be propelled by passion not invest in outcomes
> We would breathe and be charmed and amused by difference
> Be gentle and make room for every emotion

The story continues with Jake going to see two doctors who tell him that he does indeed have a rare and fatal blood disease. He is so certain that the medical professionals are "in on it," and his paranoia is so pronounced that he pulls a gun on one doctor, attempting to get him to admit that he's part of Avi and Zach's scam.

Jake comes to his senses, accepting that the doctor is in fact *not* part of any scam. We cut to a bank's safe-deposit box where Jake appears to be in a state of full resignation. He is loading his money into a bag, which he will deliver to Avi and Zach. His voice-over intones: "The only prize they guarantee you when you play this game is that you will lose. It's only a question of when."

Some may say that this is a fatalistic view, but really, Jake Green is learning a lesson in surrender. Many spiritual teachers remind us that the world is ruled by the ego, or lower self, so it is by definition a place of dysfunction. Despite this, it is possible to have a life of contentment in the ego-driven world. As Wapnick put it in his essay, "Miracles over Magic":

> "A definition that I gave many years ago for the world, which I have always liked, and refer to every once in a while, is that the world is a 'maladaptive solution to a nonexistent problem.' That is what magic is. The world is a kind of cosmic expression of the principle of magic: a 'maladaptive solution to a nonexistent problem.' It is 'maladaptive' because it does not really work (mal meaning 'bad,' and adaptive meaning 'adapting to something so as to relate to or live with it'). We thus live in the world as a way of adapting to the problem of the ego; but it does not work, because it is an attempt to solve a problem that does not exist. The world then, is an illusory solution to an illusory problem."[6]

Again, despite the world's dysfunction, many spiritual teachings remind us that we *can* live a contented life. The key is for us to let go of egoic, worldly values and to allow for our headspace to return to its natural state of peace. Our goal would be to let go of judgment, criticism, and condemnation of life's events, and let things "be" as they are. We may wonder, how this is possible? Eckhart Tolle answers this question well in his modern classic, *The Power of Now*:

> "Remember that we are not talking about happiness here. For example, when a loved one has just died, or you feel your own death approaching, you cannot be happy. It is impossible. But you *can* be at peace. There may be sadness and tears, but provided that you have relinquished resistance, underneath the sadness you will feel a deep serenity, a stillness, a sacred presence. This is the emanation of Being, this is inner peace, the good that has no opposite."[7]

The question of when Jake will lose gets answered pretty quickly. Now that he has given them all his money, Avi explains that they are "loan sharks." Jake's money is to be used as working capital for their enterprise, and Jake will serve as their henchman. The three of them visit a client, someone desperate for a short-term, usurious loan. During this interview, Jake muses in voice-over: "They say the sentence has been passed, the certificate signed. So, what's the point? The point is: This is the only option."

Jake has begun to accept his fate and starting to let go of his resistance and wise-cracking thoughts. He is beginning to adopt an "it is what it is" viewpoint. However, in regards to the money he does admit that: "I still don't like to give it away. I know I can't take it with me, so, why the pain? Why the fuck does it still hurt?"

His self-reflection continues, "What did I sign up for? Don't try to make sense out of it – not now, because it doesn't make sense. Hang the old brain up for a while, it just has been getting me into trouble anyway. Just know: if you start a job, then finish it." He doesn't realize it yet, but Jake is in the process of waking up and laying aside his ego.

This arc continues with Jake and Avi sitting down to a game of chess, while he recounts his prison experience to Avi and Zach. He tells them of his choice to spend seven years in solitary over 14 years in the general population, as well as how his cell was sandwiched between a conman and a chess master.

He goes on to say that the conman and chess master – after so many years of them considering the "ultimate" con – announced that they had found "it." Jake says, "I was under the impression that I was the clever bastard, but these boys were in a completely different class: Head tricksters of the premier division."

Then one day the conman and chess master simply vanished without taking or telling Jake, despite the fact that they had told him that they would. Adding insult to injury, when Jake eventually gets out, he discovers that they took all of his money. Having known everything about Jake from their long talks together, they knew where it was hidden.

He also told Avi and Zach of a very interesting note that was left for him after they had vanished, which said, "Rule 1: You only get smarter by playing a smarter opponent."

Jake does say of this "formula" given to him by the conman and the chess master that, "It worked. It really worked," he says, and he has used this "formula" to win big at gambling, it was how he made his second fortune.

We see Jake "working" (actually doing very unpleasant deeds) for Avi and Zach. His voice-over wonders, "Why are they dragging this on? ...They want me to suffer. These twisted bastards are making me pay – pay for my own pain." Jake does not yet realize that these unpleasant life lessons are actually in his interest. Avi and Zach are allowing him to ultimately get in touch with his own demons so he can ultimately exorcise them.

Jake sums this all up by saying, "All I want now is a little peace." He's finding that his worldly endeavors – whether of his choosing or scripted for him by Avi and Zach – are empty, unfulfilling.

It gets worse. He starts to disobey Avi and Zach when they want him to collect from people, people who cannot pay. Zach, unhappy with Jake's refusing to collect from an old lady, says: "Either they pay, or you pay." Jake shoots back, "I pay anyway," which in essence is true. Avi and Zach have taken all his money and have given him no incentives to collect from others.

Jake has been set up in his own myth of Sisyphus, condemned to roll a boulder up a hill only to see it roll back to the bottom, repeatedly forever, becoming an exercise in futility. These mean-spirited acts that Avi and Zach are having him do have no meaning for Jake. He is beginning to refine his view of "one should finish a job he has started," to one of "why start a job that is bereft of meaning?"

Now, the story takes a turn. Avi and Zach engineer a heist to steal "powder" (large amounts of drugs) from Macha by pulling his safe (that is loaded with the drugs) out of a wall. As it is done, Macha panics, as the drugs were intended for Mr. Gold, whom we never meet in the flesh, but whose name alone strikes fear in Macha.

With some twists and turns, Avi and Zach trick Macha into thinking that a rival gang, led by Lord John has stolen the drugs. A gang war begins, one that transitions cinematically into a cartoon, as the violence escalates. The choice of presenting these most violent scenes in *Revolver* as a cartoon is a bold one.

In some ways, Ritchie could be suggesting that the line between "reality" and "surreality" is thinner than we might think. By making the violence into a cartoon, Ritchie takes the edge off of the seriousness and dire consequences that seem to happen in the world, outlining for us to maybe not take it as seriously as well.

Avi and Zach's crew – including Jake – gas *both* sides, Macha's and Lord John's gangs. This enables them to complete their plan to steal Macha's money and the Lord's powder.

After their success, Jake says, "This has become a large problem, Avi."

He responds: "There's no such thing as problems, Mr. Green, only situations."

Avi can again be seen as a Holy Spirit figure for Jake's transformation. Perception is a matter of interpretation; we can label a challenging situation as a "problem," or just another "situation." He's teaching Jake that we as individuals are 100% responsible for how we interpret the events that we observe, and how we handle them.

When this masterful double heist has been concluded, Jake and Avi celebrate with yet another game of chess. As the scene begins, Zach, who is watching the game, says, "Wake up, Mr. Green." This exhortation to "wake up" is repeated several times in *Revolver*. Most spiritualities have some form of "enlightenment," or "waking up," so again we can surmise that Avi and Zach are here to encourage Jake to advance spiritually.

And, once more, Jake defeats Avi in this game of chess. Avi probes Jake on how he keeps winning. Jake explains that the idea is to let the opponent think that he's in control and that he has you on the run. Meanwhile the opponent is being set up for a fall, as you were the one in control all along.

Jake explains: "You do all the hard work, I just help you along....The more control the victim thinks he has, the less control he actually has." Rather than employing a direct, aggressive assault, the more advanced player uses *ju-jitsu*, letting the opponent's weight and aggressiveness work against himself. Jake has learned to allow the opponent to defeat himself!

On the next trip by this threesome, Jake steps out to take a call from his brother Billy, who had been doing some investigating of Avi and Zach. He tells Jake that Avi and Zach are the "last resort," notorious loan sharks who cater to the most financially desperate clientele. While this sounds on the surface to be an ominous characterization, it can be viewed in a different light. Instead, like the alcoholic hitting bottom, the Holy Spirit – or collective unconscious, if you will – often *is* the "last resort" for redemption from the depths of despair. Contrast this with "life" as we know it, where many who unwittingly listen to the voice of the ego never realize that there can be an alternative to the world of chaos because they have never hit that low point.

Jake's brother Billy goes on to outline the clout that Avi and Zach ominously wield: "[Avi and Zach] stepped on Gold's toes, and he wouldn't touch them." This makes perfect sense. Gold is also known as "Mr. Clandestine" and "Mr. Ambiguous," and is set up as a mysterious, nearly omnipotent power, who is never once encountered but greatly feared.

Gold is representative of the ego, the "other voice" in all of our heads. Ritchie further explained the character of Mr. Gold in an interview: "I like the idea that Sam Gold is a collective hallucination. He doesn't really exist but he does exist. He has no power of his own, he only has the power that you give him. He's as real as you believe him to be."[8]

Here Ritchie offers us a wonderful deconstruction of the ego. It doesn't exist, but our *belief* in the ego gives it power. The good news is that if we take away our belief in this fictional voice in our head, it deflates like a balloon of hot air.

The idea that we have two voices to which we can make a choice between is not especially novel. Dualities of Heaven/Hell, God/Devil, Right/Wrong pepper most spiritual teachings, even as it is a construct of what makes up this world of contrasts. In *Revolver*, Ritchie offers us a different perspective about the negative "voice" that some would call the "Devil," whereas others still term it the ego.

In a different interview, Ritchie elaborated:

> "I think the mind makes it more complicated than it really is. It is simply about the expression, 'You are your own worst enemy.' If you think that through a bit more, that's what this film is about. It's no more complicated than that. But it is trying to think it through, that the mind intentionally resists you being able to think it through. Why? Because it will lose its power."[9]

This is a provocative stance by Ritchie, since many a spirituality emphasize that a quiet, still mind is the road to salvation. On the other hand, there does seem to need to be *right-minded inquiry* to undo the thicket of the ego's thought system. The ego finds such inquiry highly threatening, so it disrupts meaningful thought, what Ritchie is calling thinking it through.

Billy implores Jake to "get out of there," to get away from Avi and Zach immediately. Yet, Jake does not. He re-enters the room, with no fear and a certain determination. On re-entering, he sees Avi and Zach shaking down a delinquent client. They have a gun pointed at the man, Fred, who is cowering on the floor. Avi, however, suggests that instead of Zach meting out the punishment, Mr. Green should do the deed.

Zach explains that Fred is not to be shot dead, but merely to shoot him in the back of the knee. Jake firmly refuses. His voice-over tells us: "Sometimes, a little voice tells you to think about number one. Sometimes, it's best to listen to it."

And, yet, his (non-)action differs from this message. From a "number one" perspective, Jake should comply with the order to shoot Fred. But he doesn't; instead, he turns the gun on Avi. Jake pulls the trigger, even though he finds that the gun is empty, he showed his determination and resolve by trying to shoot him.

This lesson ends with Zach unexpectedly saying, "Wake up, Mr. Green," and then he is hit in the head with a gun grip by Avi.

In the next scene a phone rings, and wake up he does. Avi tells him over the phone: "It's past the third day, and you have risen. I think you are due for a check-up."

This dialog obviously alludes to Jake being a kind of risen Jesus figure. If we extend that thought, the check up could be suggesting that Jake still needs to be tested, to ensure he is truly awake, enlightened.

Now in the next scene, we see Jake lying in bed, attended to by a little girl, his niece Rachel. She says to him: "Did the bad guys get you?"

Jake responds, "There's no such thing as bad guys, Rachel." Check. Jake is now seeing others without judgment, with no "good guys" and "bad guys." He's beginning to see the world as neutral place, and people simply as actors on a stage, playing their roles.

The film *Revolver* pushes forward. In a follow-up visit with the doctor, Jake learns that the doctor's first diagnosis was incorrect. He's still not a "well man," but he is certainly not terminal.

On leaving the doctor's office, Jake's extended voice-over reflects:

> "There is something about yourself that you don't know. Something that you will deny even exists until it's too late to do anything about it. It's the only reason you get up in the morning, the only reason you suffer the shitty boss, the blood, the sweat and the tears. This is because you want people to know how good, attractive, generous, funny, wild, and clever you really are.

> "Fear or revere me, but please think I'm special."

With this deeply introspective thought that gets down to the core of the self-serving egoic thought system, he continues:

> "We share an addiction. We're approval junkies. We're all in it for the slap on the back and the gold watch. The 'hip, hip, hoo-fucking-rah.' Look at the clever boy with the badge, polishing his trophy. Shine on, you crazy diamond. Cos we're just monkeys wrapped in suits, begging for the approval of others. If we knew this, we wouldn't do this. Someone is hiding this from us, and, if you had a second chance, you would ask: why?"

While this voice-over runs, we see two scenarios on the street play out: In the first, Jake steps off the curb and is hit by a car, his head smashing through a window. In the second, Jake steps back on the curb and the car passes with no damage done.

"If we knew this, we wouldn't do this" indeed! If we knew that we are "approval junkies," that gains us nothing, we would choose again. We would operate from our center and the "right decision" would flow seamlessly, regardless of how our words and actions might play with those around us.

As Avi and Zach drive golf balls from a rooftop high above the city with Jake watching, they pepper Jake with pedantic questions about "the game" and how to play it. Jake seems to be getting annoyed with this recurring line of questioning, and we hear his voice-over: "Don't let them play head games with you, Jake."

Avi drolly shoots back: "Is it me who's playing head games with you, Mr. Green?"

The camera whooshes up on Jake, as he turns toward Avi, recognizing that Avi can read his mind. Jake is clearly surprised by Avi's telepathic ability, as he was too preoccupied to catch it earlier.

Avi states flatly, but firmly: "You've heard that voice for so long, you believe it to be you.... You believe it to be your *best* friend."

"Do you know who Sam Gold is, Mr. Green?" Avi continues. "He's all up here," pointing to his head, "pretending to be you. You're in a game, Jake, you're in *the* game. Everyone's in this game, and nobody knows it. And all of this, this is his world. He owns it. He controls it. He tells you what to do, and when to do it."

Jake is reeling from this information that has cut to his very core and screams: "That's enough, Avi!"

Yet, Avi continues: "He's behind all the pain there ever was, behind every crime ever committed. He's hiding behind your pain, Jake. Embrace the pain, and you will win this game. Right now, he's telling you that he doesn't even exist."

With these lines, Ritchie makes a profound spiritual point. Most of us spend most of our time avoiding emotionally painful situations. We often repress painful memories through a process Freud termed sublimation. Here Avi counsels the opposite: Embrace the pain. That is, recognize and own these emotional wounds, not as a means of self-flagellation, but as a way to cleanse the mind by recognizing that these painful thoughts are unreal fabrications.

As Avi explains this, Jake's resistance spikes. His voice-over chatters loudly, wildly: "How can I be behind all the pain, all the crime, when I don't even exist?"

"We just put you to war with the only enemy that ever existed," Avi says, "and you – you think he's your best friend."

This is certainly a lot to handle, to think that "I don't even exist," as well as to be told that who you thought was your best friend (and who you considered yourself to be) is your enemy. Jake is coming to a crisis point.

After reviewing the "rules," Avi continues: "How radical are you prepared to be, Mr. Green?"

The threesome move on, but this vital sharing of knowledge continues as they drive through the city.

AVI: The more power you think you have in Gold's world, the less power you have in the Real World. You are still in prison, Jake. In fact, you never left.

Avi is not talking about his physical prison but saying that Jake has been imprisoned within his own mind and doesn't even know it! The only way to free himself is to first recognize that he has been trapped, for only then he can set about freeing himself.

And, could this "Real World" that Avi mentions be the "Real World" that Morpheus shows Neo in The *Matrix*, the world that is known after taking the Red Pill of Knowledge? The world that is perceived after the ego is dissolved and undone? There is certainly a strong case for it.

More Ritchie quotes lead us to believe that this was (more or less) his intent:

"So I like the name [*Revolver*], but I also like the concept that, if you're in a game, it keeps revolving until you realize that you are in a game and then maybe you can start evolving. The film is based on the formula of a game: where does the game start, where does it stop, and who's conning who?

"Who is the ultimate opponent? Yourself. Then comes the principle that your enemy will always hide in the last place that you would ever look. The last place you would look is inside your head and the last place you would look inside your head is behind fear. I'm not saying that formula's correct, it's just a formula and I'm interested in formulas. In this particular instance, the only opponent Jake Green has to challenge is himself by doing exactly what he doesn't want to do."[10]

Since Jake has come to certain realizations and is putting himself, the world, and money into perspective, we see the trio in a car driving to a charity. Jake has two satchels filled with money, which he casually drops off at the charity without a word of explanation to anyone.

Avi's voice-over explains: "You don't give because it's good. You give because it hurts him." We may ask, who does it hurt? When we give unconditionally and without expectation of reward, the grip of the ego – one's "Sam Gold" – is weakened in one's mind.

Now Jake gives the money to the Home for Children under Macha's name. Macha, who still is deeply in the thrall of the ego, wants to take the credit for the donation (here is another reference to the addiction for approval) even though he didn't make the contribution.

Avi, Zach, and Jake go back to the casino for "one last treat." Just by walking by a bank of slot machines they all start to pay out, with coins falling into their trays. Something has definitely changed, but what? Is this a metaphor for "hitting the jackpot?" Making the right decisions?

They settle in, and Avi tells Jake he needs to go to a meeting, and says to Jake, "Give him [Macha] what he wants. I'm sure he'll be very happy. We'll see you soon."

Cut to Macha's bedroom, with Jake standing over a sleeping Macha. The voices in his head go wild, bi-polarly swinging from "I came to apologize" to thoughts of murdering Macha, from the aggressive thoughts of "he's the enemy," to those of groveling for forgiveness. We hear Avi's voice-over saying, "Use your perceived enemy to destroy your real enemy."

As the fight in his head goes on, it settles calmly onto contrite, forgiving words: "I want you to forgive my stupidity." With that, Jake leaves Macha.

In the hallway outside Macha's apartment, Jake decides to face his fear. He closes his eyes, looking for his inner strength. He considers the stairs, but selects the elevator. As the elevator gets stuck between the 12th and 14th floors (and of course the 13th floor in and of itself is rife with meaning) this scene depicts a wonderfully ominous turn of events. The lights in the elevator fail, with dim emergency lighting setting the mood for the final "battle": Jake's "Mr. Gold" ego vs. Jake's Higher Self.

Jake's ego chatter becomes frantic with fear, irrational. Ritchie in this scene shows us Jake's ego at its most raw and his Higher Self at its most serene. He masterfully cuts back-and-forth between the two in rapid-fire succession. Jake's Higher Self says, "I can hear you. I'm onto you." Now fully exposed, Jake's ego becomes crazed and enraged; ego Jake even fakes shooting himself, only to pop back to life.

Through it all, Higher Jake realizes that his ego is not him. The Higher Jake voice-over says: "You ain't me."

Avi's voice-over has summed up the "Mr. Gold" aspect of us all very nicely: "The greatest con that he ever pulled was making you believe that he is you."

Higher Jake calmly asserts: "You're not me. You don't control me; I control you." As he comes to this realization and embraces it full heartedly, the lights go on, and the elevator proceeds down to "1," the first floor in this dreamscape. But Ritchie is telling us that, like Neo, Jake Green is now "the One." He has finally woken up; he's now enlightened.

The elevator doors open. Jake exits, clear-eyed, serene, and self-assured. As the final "test" of his resolve, Macha is there with a gun, saying: "What's your game? What's your game? Speak to me, or I'll kill you like the fucking dog that you are."

The camera cuts back to Jake. Subtle glints of light surround his head, light that wasn't there moments ago. Having chosen against violence and for forgiveness, Ritchie is showing us that Jake has ascended to a different way of being.

"Fear me," says Macha. "Fear me." He approaches Jake tentatively, but he becomes increasingly panicked himself. Macha is the representative of the "dying" ego who is trying to hang on in a last-ditch attempt to lure Jake back to its way of thinking.

This new, Higher Jake looks at him calmly, with a slight grin, eyes serene. He just walks by Macha, as if he isn't there. Showing that indeed Jake recognizes that the ego has no power, and doesn't even exist.

Back in the casino, Jake and Avi play chess once again. Avi says, "The enemy is in every one of their heads, and they trust him, because they think they are him."

We flashback to Jake reviewing his time in prison, he recalls that the conman and the chess master on either side of him had said, "You're coming with us, Jake."

But now Avi says, "We were always going take you with us, Jake, you just weren't ready to hear how hard that was going to be."

Epiphany! Avi and Zach are the chess master and conman! This entire film is a massive fantasy. Ritchie has done this all quite subtly, but when we view Avi and Zach as the Holy Spirit, or divine guidance, things fall into place. *Revolver* is the story of a man who finally listens to his Higher Self, who has set up situations (never "problems") to help him exorcise his demon ego, the Mr. Gold in all of us!

A knowing smile crosses Avi's face, as the film climaxes with Avi saying, "Checkmate." Richly, this is the first time in *Revolver* when Avi defeats Jake at chess. This could represent Jake finally lets go his need to control and gives everything over to Spirit.

Sorter

Jake Green is not the only character to wake up in *Revolver*. Although a minor character, Sorter (played by Mark Strong) wakes up as well, spontaneously so. Many reviewers noted that Sorter steals the show, and, again, this seems to be on purpose.

As the stuttering hit-man for hire, Sorter has a built-in interest for the viewer. We meet Sorter after he has been dispatched to kill Jake, and, despite his reputation as a sharp-shooter, he missed. Recall that Jake had listened to Avi and Zach, and had picked up the card that said "Pick this up." This botched hit has Sorter "out of sorts." He says: "Something is very wrong here."

Ritchie has really foreshadowed things nicely, saying, in effect, that something is rotten in Denmark. Or, like in *The Matrix*, when

Morpheus tells Neo in a less blunt way: "That there's something wrong with the world. You don't know what it is, but it's there...like a splinter in your mind, driving you mad."

Sorter's intuition is well founded, but he doesn't know what to do about it. Throughout most of *Revolver*, he's the amoral hit man, doing what he is told.

When next we see Sorter, he explains to Macha: "I-I-I-I made a mistake." Macha incredulously asks why now? Sorter answers, "Well, I-I-I-I had a bad feeling." Macha mocks the fact that Sorter has "feelings," and gets uncomfortably close to Sorter's face to emphatically hammer home the import of his assigned task.

Later, Sorter "redeems" himself as an assassin by killing two of Lord John's people. One posed as a waitress in a restaurant where Macha was dining; the other was in a car outside the restaurant.

Sorter is sent to kill more of Lord John's people, and, again, his skills prove to be impressive, his competence undeniable. All of which makes us wonder, what happened in the case of Jake Green?

However, as Macha's gang – French Paul, Sorter, and others – pay a visit on Billy, something starts to change in Sorter. He starts to quickly "sort things out." (Sorter's name is no mistake, either!)

Ritchie put it this way in an interview:

> "Sorter represents the aspect of our character in which we have taken a left-turn somewhere and later on decide that the right-turn might have been the better idea. He represents the U-turn within us when we think we've gone the wrong way or when we've decided to take a different path than the one we've been on, which is of course a terribly difficult thing to do."[11]

French Paul begins to gruesomely torture Billy, while Billy's little girl is hiding. We see that – as the torture intensifies – Sorter becomes increasingly uncomfortable. "O-O-O-OK, that's enough," he tells Paul. It seems that all it takes to transform Sorter from the amoral hitman to a person of conscience is for his eyes to open and see just how cruel French Paul is in this moment of inhuman behavior. Something snaps in Sorter's head and he makes a quick U-turn in finding his humanity.

The daughter begins to whimper, so Macha's gang find her and bring her out into the open. All assembled are about to watch Paul kill Billy in front of his daughter's eyes. Sorter cannot seem to bear this inhumanity. With the precision that he has developed throughout his deadly career, he repurposes his skills to kill all of Macha's men. One could even guess that he has put himself in "another's shoes," that he has come to a crossroad where he now relates to the daughter's terror in seeing her father about to be killed.

When he has subdued the first wave of Macha's gang, Sorter tells Billy's daughter: "None of this is real. It's just a game that the grownups are playing." Even though this is an odd thing to say, the violence in *Revolver* is often presented in this manner, a kind of unreality actively denied. This line of dialog is a foreshadowing, for – as we learn at the end of *Revolver* – the entire film depicts a massive mind game being played on Jake Green.

Once all Macha's men are killed, Sorter takes off his glasses. Symbolically, he can see, perhaps for the first time.

Dorothy Macha

Unlike Jake and Sorter, Dorothy Macha never breaks out of his unconsciousness. He is from start to finish a man who is in a constant state of fear, given to bipolar mood swings and psychopathic behavior.

The screaming question is: Why the name "Dorothy Macha"?

The name "Macha" first. It could be that Macha is a play on the word "macho." Or, perhaps, Ritchie used the name Macha as a reference to "a presumed goddess of ancient Ireland, associated with war, horses, sovereignty...."[12] Regardless, Ritchie is obviously playing games with the name "Dorothy Macha," and certainly with the first name "Dorothy," which could never be mistaken for a male name. At some level, Ritchie could be alluding to one of the most important filmic Dorothys, the one from the *Wizard of Oz*. *Revolver*, like *Oz*, is a dream, too.

Even though the character Macha seems to be over-the-top masculine, given his use of violence and angry temper, yet, at key moments in *Revolver*, Macha can go to the other extreme, by being *very* vulnerable and feminine. His dress (and undress) tends toward the dainty – often wearing a silk robe, bikini underwear, or even seen sleeping with a hair net. Nevertheless, Richie has made a very interesting character that is a study in duality and contrasts within Macha's personality, all of which is reflected in the feminine/masculine name. The viewer will, at the very least, begin to see that the crime boss is not consistently the "tough guy."

There are no romantic relationships in *Revolver*. Even though Macha and Lord John both are seen with barely dressed females, they are only there as accessories.

Lily Walker (played by Francesca Annis) is the one woman in *Revolver* that is definitely no accessory. As Gold's agent, she is arguably the strongest character in the movie. When we meet Walker, she enters like the Pope, tended to by many androgynous functionaries. Macha extends his hand to shake hers, which she ignores, getting right down to business, saying "Mr. Gold doesn't give more time, or second chances."

We can see that Macha is quite frightened by Walker and, of course, Gold. This meeting leaves him confused as to what she means by second chances. Walker's threat was vague in this first meeting; now in this second encounter her functionaries carry a wreath to "thank" Macha for his magnanimous gift to the Home for Children, despite having not completed his business with Mr. Gold. Now Macha's confusion and fear is full blown, and he tries to smooth things over by saying that everything's under control. She shuts him down, ending with "you'll be hearing from him. Good day." She turns and exits, leaving him quaking with fear.

Ritchie effectively shows how Macha's thought processes translate into words, where they alternate in rapid-fire succession from incredulity, to anger, to begging. Macha is walking on emotional eggshells, gripped with such fear that his thoughts flit about like a firefly.

Our last glimpse of Macha on the screen is him threatening Jake with a gun, standing outside of the elevator dressed in bikini briefs, literally spitting out the words, "Fear me, fear me!" Jake's response is to just walk by Macha, utterly unintimidated – unaffected! – resulting in Macha experiencing what appears to be a profound panic attack, an utter meltdown. This scene expresses very clearly how the ego, or lower self, thrives in a fearful state, and shows that Macha is exactly where Mr. Gold (the ego) wants him – dependent and confused.

A Hero's Journey
Revolver, then, is the story of Jake Green's waking up in a spiritual sense. It is no surprise that the film did not do well commercially, posing as a gangster film when in fact it is an inspired, spiritual *tour de force*, a hero's journey in the Joseph Campbell sense. *Revolver* came through a writer/director known for his ability to make aesthetic, provocative gangster movies with a British twist.

The tagline for *Revolver* is, "Your mind will not accept a game this big." That's probably true enough. But if you *believe* that it *can* accept just how big this game is, expect progress!

Rather than carp as some critics have done about the film's marketing, we should celebrate this tale. *Revolver* may well be an acquired taste, but once you start to get the riddle, it's one of those films that will stay with you for a very long time.

(See Appendix E for all the intertitles in Revolver.)

Endnotes for *Revolver*

1. Wenn, "Ritchie Denies Kabbalah Features In Revolver," Contactmusic.com, (2005), www.contactmusic.com/news-article/ ritchie-denies-kabbalah-features-in-revolver

2. Rich Cline, "Into the Mind of Revolver," Shadows on the Wall, (2005), shadows.wall.net/features/sw-rev2.htm

3. Hugh Rice, "Fatalism," The Stanford Encyclopedia of Philosophy (Spring 2013 Edition), Edward N. Zalta (ed.), http://plato.stanford.edu/archives/ spr2013/entries/fatalism/

4. Rich Cline, "Into the Mind of Revolver," Shadows on the Wall, (2005), shadows.wall.net/features/sw-rev2.htm

5. Sri Ramana Maharshi, Edited by David Godman, "Three States of Consciousness," Understanding Hinduism, www.hinduism.co.za/consciousness_the_three_states.htm

6. Kenneth Wapnick, Ph.D., "Miracles versus Magic," Foundation for A Course in Miracles, https://www.facim.org/online-learning-aids/ excerpt-series/miracles-versus-magic/part-i.aspx

7. Eckhart Tolle, *The Power of Now*, (Novato, CA: New World Library, 1999), 148

8. "Revolver: Guy Ritchie Q&A," Cinema.com, http://cinema.com/articles/3624/revolver-guy-ritchie-q-.phtml

9. B. Alan Orange, "Guy Ritchie Cons His Own Ego in Revolver," MovieWeb, (2007), www.movieweb.com/news/ exclusive-guy-ritchie-cons-his-own-ego-in-revolver

10. Raam Tarat, "Revolver," Future Movies, (2005), www.futuremovies.co.uk/reviews/revolver/raam-tarat

11. Raam Tarat, "Revolver," Future Movies, (2005), www.futuremovies.co.uk/reviews/revolver/raam-tarat

12. Wikipedia (2014), "Macha," en.wikipedia.org/wiki/Macha

Vanilla Sky: Open Your Eyes

What is a dream, and what is reality? And how would you know one from the other?

Dreaming is part of the human condition, something we all do for reasons that are not clear, biologically or even emotionally. The universality of our sleep fantasies makes it a common device in many films, and *Vanilla Sky* may make the most skillful use of dreaming since *The Wizard of Oz*.

The interesting thing is that when we dream, we are almost never aware that what is occurring in our heads is not really happening. As we dream, things seem quite real and our sleep story becomes our "reality." It is food for thought that given the fact that we don't know we're dreaming while we're asleep, who can say with certainty what is "reality," or that our waking life is not an illusion, too?

This is the field *that Vanilla Sky* plows. A remake of the 1997 Spanish film *Abre Los Ojos* (translation: Open Your Eyes), *Vanilla Sky* was written and directed by Cameron Crowe (*Almost Famous, Jerry Maguire*). It's the story of David Aames (played by Tom Cruise), a 33-year-old scion who runs the publishing empire that his father had built. By his own admission, David had been "snowboarding through life." From his perspective, he is "livin' the dream," although we later learn that "dreams" can easily become "nightmares." His *bon vivant* ways have apparently been serving him well, and yet when we meet him, his life is about to take a nosedive.

Vanilla Sky handily deconstructs along two major aspects: 1) romance and relationships and 2) metaphysical and epistemic illustration.

I. Romance and Relationships in *Vanilla Sky*
Vanilla Sky is a film that shows us a multi-layered character who struggles and ultimately succeeds in waking up from the dream. A major component of that effort to awaken is to pay attention in the classroom of life, which – for most of us – revolves around our personal relationships.

Spirituality involves both big ideas about the nature of the universe and our place in it, as well as matters of the heart, especially our close relationships. Those relationships may not be considered to be "big" issues like metaphysics or cosmology, but it can be safely said that many a spiritual path implores us to be just as mindful about our relationships – the "little" things in life – as well as the "big" things. As David says to Edmund Ventura (played by Noah Taylor) during the elevator ride near the film's end: "The little things. There's nothing bigger, is there?"

Meet the "Immortal" David Aames

In *Vanilla Sky*'s opening sequence, Crowe explains in the director's commentary track that the helicopter shots of New York City symbolize spirit "coming down to Earth." The camera pushes down toward the historic Dakota hotel, famous as John Lennon's last residence and the location for the classic film *Rosemary's Baby*.

While it's a sparkling day in New York, we hear the faint sound of a human voice that finally says the words: "abre los ojos." As the lens of the camera focuses on an apartment, the same voice is gently imploring him to "open your eyes...open your eyes."

As a worldly success story, David Aames seems to have it all: wealth, youth, good looks, a cool car, and lots of chicks. What he does not have are the "eyes to see." The eyes that have woken up to the idea that emotionally investing in material pleasures as ends in themselves does not work; it will "profit him nothing."

We meet David rising in the morning, going to the bathroom, spotting a gray hair and plucking it, subtly showing us that David is beginning a life change. Pulling the gray hair suggests the idea that David is resisting getting older, "wanting to live forever," says Crowe in the director's commentary track.

Wanting to live forever is certainly not a new notion, most of us identify with our bodies and as we watch them age, we do what we can to stave off aging and death for as long as possible. On the other hand, on a soul level, we also know that our spirit is eternal.

Identifying with the body and the ego, as does David Aames, may be the game that the world plays, but *Vanilla Sky* is a film about David getting the first glimpses of eternity. Spirit and truth and love are eternal, something we forget as we employ many delaying tactics to extend the life of the body.

Cryogenics is perhaps the most extreme example of this desire to extend the body's life. Through this process it is believed that consciousness resides in – and is inextricably linked to – the body, so if one "saves" the body, one saves one's consciousness, or personality. This is contrasted with the line by David's love interest, Sofia (played by Penélope Cruz): "I'll tell you in another life...when we are both cats." David repeats the line two times as well. It's as if a cosmic agreement has been made, and that – perhaps across nine lives – David and Sofia will be together in some form.

Torn Between Two Lovers

In the director's commentary, Crowe has a very insightful comment about societal values: "What is love in a world that's just fueled by pop culture, and a lot of visions of easy sexual conquests, and 'love' as 'sex'?

What was love – really – to us? And David Aames is a guy who's learning what love really is."

Even though the majority of religions state in various ways that "God is love," for the most part our cultural mores see love as something else. Love for us is something that people have for one another, e.g., romantic, familial, fraternal, etc.

The two women in David Aames's life give us a pretty stark contrast between what *A Course in Miracles* (ACIM) calls the "special" versus the "holy" relationship. A manifestation of the special relationship is one in which the partners use each other to meet their needs. The David/Julie (played by Cameron Diaz) relationship represents this well, in a pronounced way. We are treated early on in *Vanilla Sky* to David and Julie play-acting as a married couple. Their over-the-top faux-married-couple dialog unfolds a classic male/female dynamic, with her desperately wanting attention and him remaining non-committal. She wants to know when he will call her again, and he says "soon."

Later in the film, Julie reveals more of herself. Her insecurities burst to the surface as she suffers the indignity of being identified as David's "fuck buddy" while secretly being in love with him. She resorts to crashing his birthday party; attempts to seduce him during the party while he is circling his newfound object of desire, Sofia; and follows David and Sofia to her apartment – presumably parking all night long so as to confront him the morning after.

So lost was she that, during the party, she clings to a random waiter, draped only in a blanket. And so confused is Julie that her final act of desperation is to plunge her car off an embankment, livid with David for not reciprocating her "love" for him.

In stark contrast, Sofia displays quiet self-confidence throughout *Vanilla Sky*. She plays the idealistic girl out in the world – wide-eyed, drinking it all in. Her wit matches her sense of decency and virtue. Sofia's a modern-day Audrey Hepburn, something Crowe foreshadows for us by flashing *Sabrina* at us on the TV screen in the opening sequence of shots in David's apartment.

Crowe has remarked that with David and Sofia pleasure-delaying their first night together, it signaled the beginning of his discerning the difference between a higher form of love as opposed to his lusty, conquesting ways to date. While these are two beautiful people who are drawn to one another, their connection is not merely physical. They are, rather, soul mates, which is portrayed very well on the screen.

To be sure, the romances of *Vanilla Sky* are extreme examples, yet they are ones that we somehow can relate to. David is the hedonistic lady's man whom men admire and women want to tame.

Repetition Compulsion All Over Again

Julie could represent psychological guilt in *Vanilla Sky*. Although she dies early in the film, she keeps re-emerging, haunting David's dreams. Unless expiated, repressed guilt seems to pop up again and again in the same way – the form of manifesting guilt may shift, but the core content remains the same.

While this love relationship could be viewed as *unhealthy* in the case of the David/Julie and *healthy* in the case of the David/Sofia combination, Crowe seems to suggest a less black-and-white dividing line. For example, it's no mistake that as the film progresses, Julie becomes confused with Sofia in David's mind. In other words, there are (unavoidable?) *un*healthy aspects of the "timeless" romance between David and Sofia.

We are led to believe that the couple are, on one level, soul mates. From the moment she walks into his birthday party, he is love-struck *or* he recognizes his soul mate, or both. It is love-at-first-sight in some form or fashion, that's what Crowe and Cruise seem to want us to believe, and they pulled it off.

Crowe explains that the remake of the story required a deep connection between these two to happen fairly quickly. Another conquest by David would not do it, for he has already been there before. David and Sofia's first night together had to be somehow transcendent; they connect not so much physically, but spiritually.

The device used in *Abre Los Ojos* was to have the pair draw each other, which Crowe also used in *Vanilla Sky*. Although the exercise was to be playful for them (caricaturing each other), David instead went "deep," drawing Sofia as the soulful young woman that he saw her as. One could say that he did not just look at her lovely face or figure, but looked beyond that into her soul. This has not been his pattern in the past, womanizers like him are notorious for objectifying women.

It is also likely not a coincidence that in their first meeting, David and Sofia are wearing the same colors: Shades of red shirts and jeans. Red is often used symbolically as a color of love and passion. In looking more closely, Sofia's red shirt is brighter and clearer. David's shirt, though, is more complex...in certain light, it appears dark, almost black. In different lighting, the redness of the shirt matches more closely to Sofia's.

This small detail supports the idea that Sofia is more unconflicted, authentic, and in touch with her feelings, whereas David's feelings are definitely there but not as unconflicted as hers. He recounts to McCabe, "Somehow, I had found the last semi-guileless girl in New York City." Or, as Sofia herself says in her apartment on their first meeting: "But

I just think good things will happen if you're a good person with a good attitude. Doncha think?"

Despite this magical evening of real connection, David falls off the wagon almost immediately. On exiting Sofia's apartment, he encounters his gorgeous friend-with-benefits, Julie. She guilts him into taking a car ride with her, a drive that leads to her death and his severe disfigurement.

The Bad-Karma Boomerang

This development doesn't work out so well for David. The bad-karma boomerang always comes back to the thrower, in his case, hitting him upside the head. Julie crashes her car with both of them in it. He survives, but this poor decision on his part leads to months of painful rehabilitation. (Car crashes are called "accidents" according to the idiom, and yet this is an "accident" that is clearly not accidental!) Once ambulatory, David once again seeks out Sofia, who accepts him and his disfigured face. Unfortunately he was in too much emotional pain to accept this unconditional love from her. In essence and even after death, Julie ultimately got her way; she ruined Sophia and David's budding romance.

Prior to her death, David and Julie were overtly using one another. There was no real relationship there, just two beautiful young people getting their ya-yas out. David's use of Julie seems straightforward enough: sexual gratification with a beautiful young woman. Julie's use of David seems more complicated. She believed she loved him but didn't tell him as part of an elaborate scheme to win him over. She had even dreamed up a conclusion that sex is an unspoken promise, a promise that David was completely unaware of.

Some Yang in that Yin

It's easy to see the David/Julie pairing as unhealthy. But is the David/Sofia one a "holy" relationship? By comparison, clearly so. Cruise sells the love-at-first-sight moment well. It's easy to believe that when he sees Sofia enter his party, wrapped in a coat that looks like a cocoon, he is lit with love. Sofia emerges from that coat like a butterfly, not a "moth" as Julie branded her.

And yet Sofia may not be above catty behavior. She says of Julie that she's "the saddest girl ever to hold a martini." For "Saint Sofia" to say this about "Troubled Julie" could be a statement of compassion, or it could be a form of female competitiveness. A martini represents a good time, and so it's ironic that someone would be "sad" holding one. On the other hand, alcohol is a depressant, so it could make sense that one would be sad by drinking a martini. It's entirely possible that Sofia was a bit conflicted here, where the "saddest" statement could be both one of compassion and/or a subtle case of one-up-(wo)man-ship.

Recall, too, that Julie worried that some "clever girl" would – in effect – trick David into falling in love with her. Is Julie desperately trying to hold on to the man who is slipping away before her very eyes, or is that what Sofia has done?

The Third Wheel

At first, clearly not. Sophia has come to David's party with Brian (played by Jason Lee), David's pathetic-yet-lovable (or is he pitiful?) wing man, who draws his energy by holding on to the coattails of David as he "snowboards through life." She remained friendly – even loyal – to Brian throughout the film. For example, when Brian announces that he's leaving the party, she says, "Hang on, I'll go with you." (Brian chooses to leave alone, in a sense relinquishing any claim he had on Sofia to David.)

It is also the case that once it became clear that David was very interested in her, she did not thwart his advances. Indeed, she brought him back to her apartment. And it is Sofia who kisses David first, and then coyfully claims that she'd intended that the kiss would be on his forehead, not his lips.

The male friendship between David and Brian is also conflicted. While they do seem to be great friends on one level, David essentially steals Sofia from Brian. Brian vengefully reciprocates in a very underhanded manner. Although he denies it, it is apparent that it was Brian who spitefully told Julie (which sent her off of the rails) that all David considered her as was a "fuck buddy."

Like life itself, *Vanilla Sky* is a film about contrasts – we learn from them by observing the sometimes-frustrating contradictions and pregnant ironies of life. Brian tells David early on:

> BRIAN: – but one day you'll know what love truly is. It's the sour and the sweet. And I know sour which allows me to appreciate the sweet.

Brian often bemoans his lot in life especially when he compares it with David's. Despite Brian's gossip-mongering, this line above indicates that his general philosophy of life looks to the positive. He takes the sour in stride, knowing that no matter how dire the situation looks, he will appreciate the sweet that he knows is soon to follow. In many ways, David could have saved himself a lot of grief if he adhered to Brian's outlook.

Me and My Shadow

Life has changed radically in the past 100 years or so. There were fewer than 2 billion souls on Earth 100 years ago, now there are 7 billion. Few had electricity or running water then. Now, 2.4 billion people use the Internet, meaning that instant information at one's fingertips is available to a third of the planet today, more than the *entire population* 100 years ago.

While that *could* be a profoundly liberating thing, Crowe seems to suggest that – despite all the technological advancements – the culture still seems obsessed with the "shadow" aspects of the human condition. (In psychology, this shadow is an unconscious aspect of the personality that a person is not aware of.) Our shadow is most likely to show up when we are engaged in personal relationships.

Several have commented that *Vanilla Sky* is a Jungian film.[1] His theory about personality archetypes includes the "persona," which is the mask we present to the world. This image that we project to the world is one that often covers our true, inner self. The mask that David wears throughout much of *Vanilla Sky* is indeed an obvious nod to Jung. First presented to David by his doctors as an aesthetic patch of a sort, this "facial prosthetic" later becomes his crutch.

David undergoes experimental surgery in which his face is fixed. Sofia peels the mask off his face revealing the handsome visage he had prior to the accident with Julie. For the time being, David no longer uses the mask. However, once he has been arrested for murder, he puts the mask back on. In order to cope with this nightmare, it seems David regresses and hides behind the mask. Having lost his grip on reality, the mask seems to comfort and protect him.

His narrative further runs amok and he ends up going to prison and finds that he and those around him can't seem to discern who Julie is and who Sofia is. At one point deep into *Vanilla Sky*, the evidence seems to be that Julie is now Sofia and Sofia is now the dead Julie. So confusing is all this that it lands him in prison for suffocating Diaz's character, who is now named Sofia, not Julie.

Expiating the guilt that generates our shadow persona seems no easy task, but this masterpiece of a film points us in the direction to use our *relationships* to start to see our blind spots in order for them to be addressed. If we "keep our eyes open" and commit to being a "good person with a good attitude" that Sofia suggests as a way of being – we can make significant spiritual progress.

II. The Metaphysics and Epistemology of *Vanilla Sky*

Under the billing of a modern Hollywood romantic/sci-fi movie, *Vanilla Sky* has a cosmology that one sees in Eastern thought, meaning Buddhist or Hindu. Unlike most Western, Abrahamic religious traditions, Eastern thought often comes from the standpoint that the universe is an entire, integrated entity. Although this "oneness" visually has a multiplicity of parts, according to these traditions this is just an *appearance*, an illusion. Even as this Great Tapestry called life may have different colors and patterns in it, it is still a single sheet of cloth.

Certainly this so-called dream of time and space seems real enough to us, and plays out as an elaborate drama in our lives. But, as we peek inside David Aames's world, we are led through a storyline that we discover is a dream within a dream.

Deeply spiritually themed films don't necessarily become box-office sensations, although *Vanilla Sky* was in fact profitable, perhaps on the strength of the cast of Cruise, Cruz, and Diaz. Reviewers generally did not find *Vanilla Sky* to be all that, dismissing it with words like "incoherent." When a film is non-linear in story and metaphysical in perspective, film critics are apt to misunderstand and pan the work.

In some ways, *Vanilla Sky* is less a "movie" and more of a "filmic experience." Viewed in this way, a filmic experience becomes a different art form. It is one that encourages us to view the film multiple times, each time gaining subtle nuances that the director has embedded within it. Here are a number of what Crowe called "clues" that cue us in to the dreaming metaphysics of the film:

- He purposely put on TV in David Aames's apartment Audrey Hepburn in *Sabrina*, a film he characterizes as "the dream of romance."

- More than once we see the album cover of *The Freewheelin' Bob Dylan*, a highly romantic image. That image is even recreated with David and Sofia on a street with a VW van and similar period cars parked on it.

- Crowe carefully calculated the dream sequence of David driving a black Ferrari on the abandoned streets of New York. David runs through an empty Times Square, with each image on the billboards representing a "quick fix." Much whooshes by us in that scene, including one of the electronic billboards in Times Square playing an episode of *The Twilight Zone* entitled "Shadow Play." The director noted that an empty Times Square would be where a person would feel "most alone," or most separate. All this material wealth, but with no one to share with seems a most empty existence. In a way, David is soul-less, and the unpeopled Times Square is his unconscious mind telling him so.

- There are several Beatles themes that run through the entire film:

  - The opening shot of The Dakota, where John Lennon last lived.

  - McCabe and David have a discussion about which Beatle they prefer.

  - Paul McCartney wrote the song *Vanilla Sky* for the project. It plays over the credits.

  - Crowe reports that he had planned to use "Strawberry Fields" in the soundtrack, but that didn't quite work.

- The window sticker on David Aames's Mustang reads "02 30 01," which is not a real date since there are never 30 days in February, subtly saying that this whole sequence could never have happened. The entire film is a dream, even the real-seeming storyline.

- In the first prison-cell scene with David and McCabe (played by Kurt Russell), Crowe notes that there is a TV playing *To Kill a Mockingbird*. He put it here to point to the idea that *Vanilla Sky* is about "the psyche of a man" and to remind us that "everything matters."

- The John Coltraine hologram in David's apartment during his party, is yet another clue that what is going on is a dream, or will be at some point. It has been said that the universe is holographic, that each part contains the whole (which in turn contains the parts!) The holographic image of Coltraine soulfully playing his saxophone gives us a glimpse into some of the hidden messages of *Vanilla Sky*. When Sofia passes her hand through the hologram of Coltraine, his image keeps playing without missing a beat. By this movement of her hand, we get to see the metaphysics of a hologram in action and understand how this idea works. The oneness is undisturbed by the apparent movement of the parts in the whole, even though there can be disturbances in the image, still the whole remains complete.

Tech Support!

The dream within the dream may not be obvious at the outset of *Vanilla Sky*, but unfolds slowly in key scenes throughout the movie by a character named Ventura, otherwise known as Tech Support.

As the film crescendos and climaxes at the end, Ventura explains that most of David's "life" has not happened. Instead, his body has been cryogenically frozen and his mind is being treated to the "Lucid Dream" package that Life Extension (L.E.) has offered him during his long period of suspended animation.

This extended Lucid Dream has been "monitored," according to Ventura, and we kind of get the sense that the life lessons that David Aames experiences in his Lucid Dream are designed to wake him up. In a way, he has woken *himself* up, by way of a *self-correcting contract with Life Extension*! In fact, the word "wake" appears in the script of *Vanilla Sky* 11 times. The phrase "open your eyes" appears nine times.

The act of dreaming is widely considered vital to emotional health, and many Western psychologists and sleep scientists believe that we "work things out" in our dreams. Social challenges we face sometimes show up – often symbolically. The Buddhist idea of Lucid Dreaming takes this idea to another level. Originally a Buddhist practice, Lucid Dreaming is now performed by many spiritual aspirants in many traditions, where the skill to remain lucid while dreaming is cultivated. If we can be trained to directly manipulate and remain lucid during our dreaming state, there is no telling how far we can go in alleviating emotional pain, for in this process we are consciously manipulating the unconscious for the greater good of our wellbeing.

(Technically, then, the L.E. Lucid Dream package is *not* classic lucid dreaming, since David in this case is not consciously in control of what happens to him in his cryogenic fantasy world.)

On another level, some believe that even our waking life is an elaborate dream that is playing out in its own format. For example, in Hinduism, it is believed that Maya – the world of time and space – is also an illusion, things are not what they appear. If – for a moment – we take this to be true, then by extension, if we are having a lucid dream that takes us to another time and place while we are asleep in bed, why could we then not be lucid dreaming while we are "awake"?!

"You are Their God."

Perhaps the most metaphysically poignant moment in *Vanilla Sky* is when Ventura approaches David in a bar/restaurant. Ventura, serving as a kind of Holy Spirit guiding figure, stands outside of the moment looking in – gently but forcefully explaining to David that he has the ability to make his world as he wants it. In fact it has been said, he (and we!) are always doing so. Metaphysically speaking, Ventura reminds us that we each co-create our world *because we are 100% in charge of our perceptions and interpretations*. We may think we have no power, but ultimately it is all in our hands, or more accurately, in our minds.

Ventura shows up a few times in the film, but only when David starts to really become unhinged does Ventura make himself known to him.

The illusory world, Maya, is revealed to David Aames in the restaurant scene. At this point, the difference between sleeping and waking is blurred for him, and he is thrown into a state of profound confusion where he is unsure of what is real and what is not.

Ventura says to David:

> VENTURA: David, look at these people. It seems as though they're chatting away, doesn't it? Nothing to do with you – and yet, they might only be here because you wanted them to be. You are their God. And not only that, you could make them obey you... or even destroy you.
>
> DAVID: What I'd like them to do is shut up! Especially you!

In that moment, everyone in the room freezes, and all sound ceases, all movement stops. This is a great lesson for a very surprised David; he sees here that his anger and sense of victimization by others is not justified, for *he* is the one in control. It's quite clear that Ventura is correct: David is their God, or their maker. In this moment, he appears to be omnipotent!

"Life is but a Dream."

Many little things in *Vanilla Sky* point to the film as being a dream. For example, in the opening scene in David's apartment, Julie's cell phone rings, and its ring tone is the melody for the song "Row, Row, Row Your Boat." This childhood song is one that is in fact very metaphysical and has snuck in the back door of our childhood nursery rhymes. We were subconsciously taught early on that as we navigate the journey of life, or the stream of consciousness – to be merry, for "life is but a dream." We adults forget the attitude of light-hearted happiness as we take ourselves and our lives incredibly seriously, painfully so.

Could we all be dreaming up our lives, populating our own dreamscapes with dream characters, including – ultimately – our "self," or more properly, our identity as a separate person? Even as there is no empirical evidence that this is so, it is a metaphysical story that lets our imaginations soar.

For Every Action There is an Equal and Opposite Reaction
Ramana Maharshi's inquiries would ask, "Who am I?", and the answer is not all that obvious. We can ask ourselves that question repeatedly, but any answer we come up with is not verifiable.

By all indications, based on our (fleeting) perceptions, the world is governed by cause and effect. In the physical world Newton's Law is validated over and over again: "For every action there is always an equal and opposite reaction."

Newtonian physics seems serviceable enough. To drive a nail into wood, we swing a hammer, and the task is done. Hammering is a relatively neutral-to-positive act. We tend to associate "building" with "improving life in some way."

And, yet, it's also the case that productive acts are deemed "productive" entirely by *interpretation*. A new building may or may not be helpful, e.g., the acts of building a Habitat for Humanity home versus building a Nazi prison camp. These two structures involve the same basic activities but the interpretation of their use and purpose vary widely.

The point that is being made is that events in our lives are up to our individual *interpretations*. Everything is neutral until a judgment is cast upon it, since everything is filtered through our own individual perceptual lens, a lens more or less clogged with the mud of our biases, judgments, and preconceived notions. David's (and our) journey is one that is comprised of clearing away the clouded vision of misperception and waking up to reality.

The Eye of the Beholder
There is no inherent reason that David would be irritated with Ventura or the diners in that bar/restaurant. His mood created that sense of irritation that he had in that moment. Had he been in a better state of mind, he might have felt enlivened by the atmosphere, or even tuned out all of their voices had he been, for example, in the company of Sofia.

This is reminiscent of the profound line from ACIM: "This is not done to me, but I am doing this,"[2] meaning that every moment in our life is a choice. As we make those choices, we are responsible for the *interpretation* that we have placed on that choice and therefore are responsible for everything that goes on around us and how it is out-pictured.

It has now come to the great choice-point for David as Ventura summarizes:

VENTURA: It is now your moment of choice. You can return to your Lucid Dream, and live a beautiful life with Sofia, or whomever you wish...or you can choose the world out there.

He alludes to the idea that the client's dream is always benign, and is being "monitored" by what he calls "your panel of observers" who are eternally "waiting for you to choose." He indicates that when the choice is made by you, the observers will fill in the dreamscape to your specifications. (Unless, of course, it develops a glitch, which in this case he would fix if David so chooses.)

Finally in conclusion he says:

VENTURA: It's been a brilliant journey of self-awakening, and you've simply got to ask yourself – what is happiness to you?

(It's no mistake that this question about happiness is the same one that Julie asks David moments before she drives off the embankment!)

More or less ignoring Ventura's points, David now responds with the matter that concerns him most and is at the forefront of his mind:

DAVID: I want to live a real life. I don't want to dream any longer.

This is someone who now wants to take responsibility for his life. Because he had previously given away his responsibility, he's now in a position to make an informed choice, and he decides to take back his power of decision.

This is the chronology of *Vanilla Sky*'s storyline:

1. Where David is living in an unconscious manner, drifting and living the high life. After the accident, this unconscious living roughly includes up to the point of his falling asleep on the street in Sofia's neighborhood. He literally has hit bottom, a broken, disfigured man.

2. David begins to awaken from his unconscious frame of mind after hitting bottom. It might be termed his "wake up call." He discovers and opts for Life Extension (L.E.) by deciding to commit suicide. He now experiences an elaborate dream life while his body is in a cryogenic tank, but he doesn't remember that he made the choice for the dream.

It seems that a glitch in the program occurs, (maybe it is the unconscious not wanting to be in a dream anymore and trying to wake up) so his dream becomes a nightmare. In fact, at one point, David says, "Everything is a nightmare." Indeed, the word "nightmare" appears seven times in the script. This nightmare becomes so pronouncedly unpleasant that Ventura needs to intervene in the dream to either have David make the choice to keep on dreaming or to get him to face his residual fear – in his case, the fear of heights so that he can wake up.

The Ah-Ha Moment

Midpoint in the film, David starts to wake up to awareness when McCabe leaves the prison cell for what is supposed to be the last time. Upon departing, McCabe had asked who "Ellie" was, and young Aames didn't recall the name. David has an epiphany, though, when he sees a commercial for L.E., or Life Extension, through the window of the guard's booth. He recognizes the name "Ellie" to be "L.E." Something is starting to awaken in David now; the pieces are beginning to fall into place.

His dialogs with McCabe will begin to change, but in the past they have been somber, evasive, and filled with deflections and obtuse musings. He had come across to McCabe as deranged and unbalanced.

While McCabe doesn't quite say what David's problem is, we are led to believe that his "Daddy" issues may have been far more pronounced than had been recognized by even David himself. The floor-to-ceiling portrait of his father in David's apartment suggests a continuing domination of the son by his deceased larger-than-life father.

Crowe economically alludes to the "Daddy issue" theory when he has McCabe quote from the elder Aames book, *Defending the Kingdom*:

> MCCABE: I've read it. Page 127. "David Junior was a delight as a child." Did I miss something here? Is that all he wrote about you?

David deflects in his response:

> DAVID: I don't think he ever got over the fact that I was terrified of heights.

Aames Senior was fabulously successful by worldly standards, and an adventurer who took to the skies – a man who skydived and ballooned. In keeping with Freud's classic reaction formation, David Junior developed acrophobia; psychologically this was a way to deal with a dominating authority figure. In Aames Senior's kingdom, the

Prince being afraid of heights would seem especially disappointing to a daredevil such as himself.

As Joseph Campbell (whose work on the hero's journey and myths continues to be a great influence for Hollywood storytelling), has said: "The cave you fear to enter holds the treasure you seek." This wonderfully rich metaphor speaks volumes for the character of David Aames. He needs to delve into the cave of his subconscious to face his fears, in this case, his fear of heights. When and if he does so, he will find his treasure, his freedom from the bondage that has limited his mind.

We now see that Aames Junior has developed acrophobia as a reaction to his father's dominating insistence that his son has the same interests and drive that he has. David's rebellion is a search for selfhood, independence from his father. The problem is that everything that David now has – his lifestyle of high living and all that goes with it – is because of his father; his whole setup is not anything that he has attained on his own. The guilt of this psychological dichotomy runs him in the opposite direction. He has a fear of heights (a subconscious rebellion against his father) and he jeopardizes his father's business by being a careless, carefree playboy. He does not take responsibility for his situation and blames the other members of the board (dubbed by him as "the seven dwarfs") for any and all calamities.

Nightmares are Dreams, Too

Not long after the accident, as everything comes crashing down around the young Aames's disfigured body, he is still not ready to "go into the cave" and face his fears, so he opts for the "happy dream" by going to L.E. Unfortunately for him (or maybe not so unfortunately), the dream runs a glitch (which is really his subconscious seeping out into the dream as a wake-up call) and his happy dream turns into a nightmare. He believes he has killed Sofia (who he thought was Julie) and ends up in prison under the care of a psychologist. It's interesting how his mind has made the prison a "holding cell" where he can work out the puzzle of his life and gain the strength to do what has to be done.

He had thought that he could escape from his ruined life (even as it was only himself who thought it was ruined) by going into an eternal dream. If his psychological framework was different (i.e., if he hadn't relied so heavily on his looks as being his identity, for example), he could have still lived a productive, full life. But as all things psychological, everything must run its course.

The only way for him to escape from this nightmare was that he had to finally confront his fears – his subconscious mind demanded it. This feat was represented at the end of the movie by him making the choice to either not jump off of a skyscraper (stay in the dream) or to jump (take back the reins of his own life and wake up).

At the conclusion of this film, we see the choice that he has made, for we hear a woman's voice saying: "Relax... relax, David... open your eyes..." An eye then does open on screen, suggesting that David has indeed awoken from the dream state. So Ventura's story was correct; David had been cryogenically frozen for 150 years. During that time his Lucid Dream had gone awry, becoming a nightmare. But now by having faced his fear *within* his nightmare, he woke up *from* the nightmare.

Or, as McCabe has put it to him: "Do you understand that you hold the keys to this prison?" Psychologically, fear – in all of its various forms – is a prison for one's mind, but it also is a product of the mind – an invention of the mind, in fact. Even as we hold onto the fears that grip us, we always have the means to escape them. When we are ready – as David Aames *was* ready – they can be confronted. When we do let our fears go, we set ourselves free by seeing their powerlessness over us.

The Music of *Vanilla Sky*

Of course, any deconstruction of *Vanilla Sky* would be incomplete without a discussion of the film's soundtrack. Crowe being the director makes the final music selections, so a little bit about his background is necessary. He came to prominence as a writer for *Rolling Stone* magazine, and his film *Almost Famous* represented a semi-autobiographical account of his history in the music world. His wife, Nancy Wilson, was in the band Heart. She composed some of the original music for *Vanilla Sky* – the song on the CD by Julianna Gianni (Julie), "I Fall Apart." This is the tune that she played for David moments before she crashes her car.

Crowe tells the story of how Paul McCartney visited the set of *Vanilla Sky* while he was in the midst of recording a new album. He offered Crowe the song *Vanilla Sky,* which plays while the film credits roll.

One of the more poignant music selections for *Vanilla Sky* was "Solsbury Hill" by Peter Gabriel. While this light-feeling tune played during the scene when David and Sofia sketch each other, a closer read of the lyrics reveals Gabriel sharing a profound moment of awakening. In a frequently used metaphor for a heavenly Nirvana on earth, the lyrics reveal a moment where he was beckoned "Home":

> Climbing up on Solsbury Hill
> I could see the city light
> Wind was blowing, time stood still

Eagle flew out of the night
He was something to observe
Came in close, I heard a voice
Standing stretching every nerve
Had to listen had no choice
I did not believe the information
I just had to trust imagination
My heart going boom boom boom
"Son," he said "Grab your things,
I've come to take you home."

Another musical decision that was made for *Vanilla Sky* that subtly points to the film having a metaphysical bent was to have David Aames sing the Joan Osbourne song, "If God Was One of Us." In that sequence, as he's being wheeled into the operating room to reconstruct his disfigured face, David sings out loud to himself:

What if God was one of us
Just a slob like one of us
(Just a stranger on the bus)
Trying to make his way home

While some may find these lyrics sacrilegious, they could also easily refer to the more Eastern thought that we are each one with God. Rather than God being put on a distant pedestal in Heaven, this song could be portraying God in the here and now, in all things and in all beings, even within a "slob" like us.

This Eastern view of oneness could even be seen to parallel the Bible, where Jesus said in the New Testament, "Neither shall they say, lo here! or, lo there! for, behold, the kingdom of God is within you." (Luke 17:21, KJV).

Although Christian interpretations vary, Jesus stated that the miracles he performed were not reserved only to himself. He said that we also had the ability to perform miracles because we have the faith of the Kingdom within us.

"Verily, verily, I say unto you, He that believeth on me, the works that I do shall he do also; and greater works than these shall he do; because I go unto my Father." (John 14:12, KJV).

It should be no surprise that *Vanilla Sky* is imbued with spiritual symbolism. In an interview on BeliefNet.com, Crowe revealed among other things that he is a practicing Catholic.[3] In that interview, Crowe says:

"My parents really did let me know that compassion and kindness – not necessarily given with an agenda – is a great way to live your life. So I've always tried to do that, and it's communicated in the work that I've done. Sometimes people can be pretty nasty in the way they respond to something I've done in a movie. And it's good to take it for what it is and move on and just know that you have a certain compassion for people in general – that includes naysayers. Because you're really just on a journey to do the best you can and maybe leave things a little better off than when you got here. And that's the basic way my parents raised me and the way I'll be raising our kids."

Interestingly, the only musical artist's work who appears twice in the film is R.E.M. ("All the Right Friends" and "Sweetness Follows") The band shares its name with REM sleep, which is the rapid-eye-movement we experience during our dreams. Coincidence? Perhaps, or Crowe may be subtly reminding us – again – that *Vanilla Sky* is but a dream.

"Every passing moment is a chance to turn it all around."
The spiritual quest is no simple, cut-and-dried matter. Much as we would like to follow a specific practice to a T – strike the "right" yoga pose, say the "right" prayer, do the "right" good deed – it's just not so simple. Sainthood evades virtually everyone, with Jesus and Buddha being the very largest of exceptions.

And, yet, Sofia also had it right: "Every passing moment is a chance to turn it all around." Every passing moment is a new opportunity. *Vanilla Sky* reminds us that it is *this* next moment that deserves our attention, for it is in *this* next moment that we might just wake up from this nightmare.

Perhaps *this* is the moment?!

Endnotes for *Vanilla Sky*

1. Carlo Cavagna, "Vanilla Sky," About Film.com, (2001), www.aboutfilm.com/movies/v/vanillasky.htm

2. *A Course in Miracles*, (Glen Ellen, CA: Foundation for Inner Peace, 1992) T-28.II.12:5

3. "Cameron Crowe: A Positive Spin on Life," BeliefNet.Com, (2005), www.beliefnet.com/Entertainment/ Movies/2005/10/ Cameron-Crowe-A-Positive-Spin-On-Life.aspx

Reel Vision

Appendix A: Plato's Cave

Allegory of the Cave
Partially excerpted from Wikipedia, the free encyclopedia[1]

"The Allegory of the Cave (Analogy of the Cave, Plato's Cave, Parable of the Cave) is presented by the Ancient Greek philosopher Plato in [his book] *The Republic*...
"Plato has Socrates describe a gathering of people who have lived chained to the wall of a cave all of their lives, facing a blank wall. The people watch shadows projected on the wall by things passing in front of a fire behind them, and begin to designate names to these shadows. The shadows are as close as the prisoners get to viewing reality. He then explains how the philosopher is like a prisoner who is freed from the cave and comes to understand that the shadows on the wall do not make up reality at all, as he can perceive the true form of reality rather than the mere shadows seen by the prisoners."
The philosopher has unloosed the chains (of his mind) and is able to see through the illusions that others have taken for reality. He is then said to have gone out of the cave into the light, and comes back to tell the chained ones that freedom is at their fingertips.
It is also an interesting parallel as to how similar Plato's Cave is to a darkened movie theatre, with the fire behind the people (projector) casting images onto a blank wall (screen).

---

[1] http://en.wikipedia.org/wiki/Allegory_of_the_Cave

Appendix B: Further Reflections on *The Matrix*

Recall that in this volume's deconstruction of *The Matrix*, Morpheus presents to Neo one of the deepest questions that exists, and that is, "What is real? How do you define real?"

For most of us reality is the phenomenal world, that is, the world we experience through our five senses. However, Morpheus introduces the idea that our senses are "simply electrical signals interpreted by your brain." We may believe that our eyes see or our ears hear but, according to Morpheus, we are incorrect. They don't! Instead, our sensory organs are just that: sensors that give information to the mind. They are the bridge between the world's phenomena and our minds, and without which we would be deaf, blind, and dumb. This idea is played out masterfully as we see the crew having seemingly real experiences in the world even as they are hooked into a chair.

Biologically, the brain is where these electrical signals are processed and labeled. For example, the brain might label a massage as "pleasant," but if the massage therapist presses too hard, a pain threshold is breached and the pressure is labeled "pain." The level of the threshold will vary by the individual as well.

Interestingly, from a biological perspective, the images on the human retina are upside down. The brain translates the images we see into right-side-up pictures that we label our "vision."

It is important to note that Morpheus does not advocate to not trust the senses, but to go about business in the world with the recognition that what is seen, heard, or felt is somewhat distorted and incomplete, and even upside down! In other words, it is not to be relied on as the be-all and end-all, we can keep an open mind about the world around us and still recognize that none of us is all-knowing.

As we interpret these signals, we come to realize that they are all *interpretations*. That interpretation is subject to the learned biases that we carry around with us. "Beauty," for example, is not really in the "eye of the beholder," it's in the *head* of the beholder. Of course, even the head is not exactly true, since consciousness's locality is impossible to know. We may well think we think with our brains, but even that is simply not provable!

For many, this is a bracing concept. Conventional wisdom and science tell us that *obviously* consciousness is in the head. But if one employs the self-inquiry techniques of, say, Byron Katie, it is hard not to at least *question* where the source of knowledge rests.

Not to belabor the point, but if one asked the simple question, "How do I know that I think with my brain?" one could respond: "Scientists say so." But a scientist's opinion is not proof *for you*; it's deferring to an authority. One could be more honest and say: "My thoughts seem to originate in my head." We might probe that a bit more deeply, and ask: "Yes, they seem to be in your head, but do you *absolutely know* that they originate in your brain?"

The honest answer is, "No, I don't absolutely know that."

No matter what one's opinion is of where the source of consciousness resides, one can look at it as an exercise for the mind, and in many ways it *is* a mind game. Many report that these sorts of cognitive gymnastics help to free one's consciousness by thinking outside the box. It's also radically honest. We have unconsciously accepted conventional wisdom as our own, despite the fact that conventional wisdom is often overturned when new paradigms explode old assumptions, ones that are based on ultimately false premises.

As *A Course in Miracles* tells us, "words are but symbols of symbols." It's important to keep that in mind when considering these non-dualistic concepts. Non-dualistic thought comes from the metaphysical standpoint that "the world is an illusion," literally unreal. This premise of non-duality arises from the understanding that everything is united within one whole framework, that there literally cannot be two of anything. If there is the perception of two, then one is perceiving unreality, because there are no contrasts within eternal unchanging love.

In a sense, *The Matrix* follows along dualistic lines, since Thomas Anderson's "life" was a complete fabrication, even the thoughts that he considered his own *did not* begin in his head but were being fed to him by the AI machines! His so-called life was literally unreal in all ways.

Another prominent non-dualist, Eckhart Tolle, author of *The Power of Now*, was once asked, "Is the world real or unreal?"

Tolle replied: "It's a temporary manifestation of the real."

A way to frame this is to say that things are as they are. The material world is *temporarily* real; the universe is in flux and constantly changing. In any given moment, however, it is real enough. However, the point being made here is that it is our *interpretations* that are all imaginary and have no existence. The human being cannot figure out, resolve, or even understand what reality is because it is *human consciousness* that is not real. A real mind-bender, for sure.

From another angle, there is much truth in the statement: "Perception is reality." This is certainly true for the perceiver making the statement. This widely used statement was shortened from, "Perception is merely reality filtered through the prism of your soul." This original quote is more poetic and accurate, for it recognizes that human perception colors and, in a sense, co-creates what a person believes reality to be, not what reality actually is. In recalling the previous discussion about interpretation, one could even say that "perception is interpretation."

Some philosophers contrast *phenomenon* (how objects or events *appear* to the senses) with *noumenon* (what objects or events actually are without the use of the senses). This phenomenon/noumenon differentiation is a way that we can recognize that the physical world exists, but that because humans interpret the physical world through the senses and the mind, we ultimately cannot really know the noumenon.

Appendix C: Gnosticism

Gnosticism was essentially a branch of early Christianity that posited the idea that the realization of "Gnosis" (knowledge) is the way to bring about the soul's salvation from the material world. The Gnostics believed the material world was created through an intermediary being called the "demiurge," rather than directly by the supreme universal God.

In most branches of Gnosticism, the demiurge was considered imperfect or even evil, but nevertheless clearly anthropomorphic. The problem was that humans were spiritual entities that were trapped in bodies, and the only way to liberate them was by receiving and understanding the secret gnosis, or knowledge.

The Gnostics believed that a spiritual being must come from the other side to awaken humans from their spiritual slumber. The spirit in humans was believed to be asleep, and people needed to be reminded that their true identity resides within the Supreme Being.

The messenger from the other side (thought by early Christian Gnostics to be Jesus Christ) holds the key to salvation. He had the secret knowledge, which he taught his disciples, who in turn passed it on to others. In short, they believed that Jesus was a messenger who came to the world to remind people who they really were and to teach them how to return to home to God.

There were many differences among the Gnostic sects concerning Jesus. Some thought he was the Supreme Being incarnate who came to bring gnosis to earth. Others adamantly denied that the Supreme Being came in flesh, claiming that Jesus was merely a human who attained divinity through gnosis and taught his disciples to do the same. These are the ones who took Jesus' statement from the New Testament literally when he said: "Neither shall they say, Lo here! or, lo there! for, behold, the kingdom of God is within you." In other words, the Kingdom is as accessible to us as it was to him if we were devoted to the single-minded pursuit of God consciousness.

Further, in the mythology of Gnosticism, it is the demiurge who created the material world and is believed by humanity (erroneously) to be "reality." The only reality that has any validity is outside of the material universe and is with the Supreme being. The goal is to arrive at that point of knowledge by gnosis.

According to several writers who advocated that *Dark City* had a Gnostic bent, they paralleled the character in *Dark City*, John Murdoch, to the messenger coming from the other side to bring humanity gnosis. He awakens from his spiritual slumber and eventually awakens those around him. The Strangers in *Dark City* then would be symbolic of the demiurge spoken of in Gnosticism.

Appendix D: Two Versions of *Dark City*

It is an interesting aside to note that there are two versions of *Dark City*, the theatrical release and the director's cut. In the theatrical release, we hear a voice-over and screen roll of these words:

> "First there was darkness. Then came the strangers. They were a race as old as time itself. They had mastered the ultimate technology. The ability to alter physical reality by will alone. They called this ability 'Tuning'. But they were dying. Their civilization was in decline, and so they abandoned their world seeking a cure for their own mortality. Their endless journey brought them to a small, blue world in the farthest corner of the galaxy. Our world. Here they thought they had finally found what they had been searching for."

Reportedly, the studio insisted on this introduction in the theatrical version since it was not present in the director's cut. They felt that the storyline would be too complex for viewers otherwise.

Appendix E: Intertitles in *Revolver*

The greatest enemy will hide in the last place you would ever look.
- Julius Caesar 75 BC

The only way to get smarter is by playing a smarter opponent.
- Fundamentals of Chess 1883

First rule of business, protect your investment.
- Etiquette of the Banker 1775

There is no avoiding war, it can only be postponed to the advantage of your enemy.
- Niccolo Machiavelli 1502

The only real enemy to have ever existed, is an eternal one.
-The Road to Suicide, pg 1, line 1

Your friends are close, but your enemy is closer.
- The Road to Suicide, pg 1, line 2

Reel Vision

Bibliography

A Course in Miracles, 2nd Edition, Foundation for Inner Peace, 1996

Be as You Are: The Teachings of Sri Ramana Maharshi, Sri Ramana Maharshi and David Godman, Compass, 1989

I Am That, Sri Nisargadatta Maharaj, The Acorn Press, 1973

Loving What Is: Four Questions That Can Change Your Life, Byron Katie and Stephen Mitchell, Three Rivers Press, 2003

Spiritual Cinema, Gay Hendricks and Stephen Simon, Hay House, 2005

Spiritual Enlightenment: The Damnedest Thing, Jed McKenna, Wisefool Press, 2002

Spiritual Warfare, Jed McKenna, Wisefool Press, 2011

Tao Te Ching, Lao Tsu, translated by Gia-Fu Feng and Jane English, Vintage Books, 1972

The Hero with a Thousand Faces, Joseph Campbell, Princeton University Press, 1972

The Direct Path, Greg Goode, Non-Duality Press, 2012

The Movie Watcher's Guide to Enlightenment, David Hoffmeister, Living Miracles Publications, 2003

The Power of Now, Eckhart Tolle, New World Library, 1999

If you enjoyed this book

and want to learn more,

visit us at Reel-Vision.Webs.com

www.ingramcontent.com/pod-product-compliance
Lightning Source LLC
LaVergne TN
LVHW011331080426
835513LV00006B/285